It's A Good Day

by

Dianne M. Larsen

It's A Good Day

ISBN 978-0-934523-83-7

Library of Congress Control Number: 2022910403
© Copyright by Dianne M. Larsen 2022

Publisher's Cataloging-in-Publication data

Names: Larsen, Dianne M., author.
Title: It's a good day / by Dianne M. Larsen.
Description: Hills, IA: Middle Coast Publishing, 2022.
Identifiers: LCCN: 2022910403 | ISBN: 978-0-934523-83-7
Subjects: LCSH Affirmations. | Self-talk. | Peace of mind. | BISAC SELF-HELP / Affirmations | SELF-HELP / Anxieties & Phobias | SELF-HELP / Meditations | SELF-HELP / Motivational & Inspirational | SELF-HELP / Self-Management / Stress Management
Classification: LCC BF637.P3 L37 2022 | DDC 152.4/6--dc23

Cover: Licensed Shutterstock.com image: Ukrainian summer, sunrise in the mountains with blooming rhododendrons, by Rushov.

MIDDLE COAST PUBLISHING

Good Books Are Where We Find Our Dreams

Namaste

The word is a customary manner of respectfully greeting and honoring a person or group, appropriate to be used at any time of the day or night.

A MEMORY

I woke up very early, before the sun arose.
Tiptoed to the window,
to the pane pressed my nose.

I could see through the glass,
falling flakes of white.
The world had transformed.
Working through the night.

My bare feet were icy cold.
So back to bed I went.
Jumped under covers quick,
as if by the devil sent.

I snuggled in the blankets.
Closed my eyes, then slept.
And tucked away forever
a memory I treasure yet.

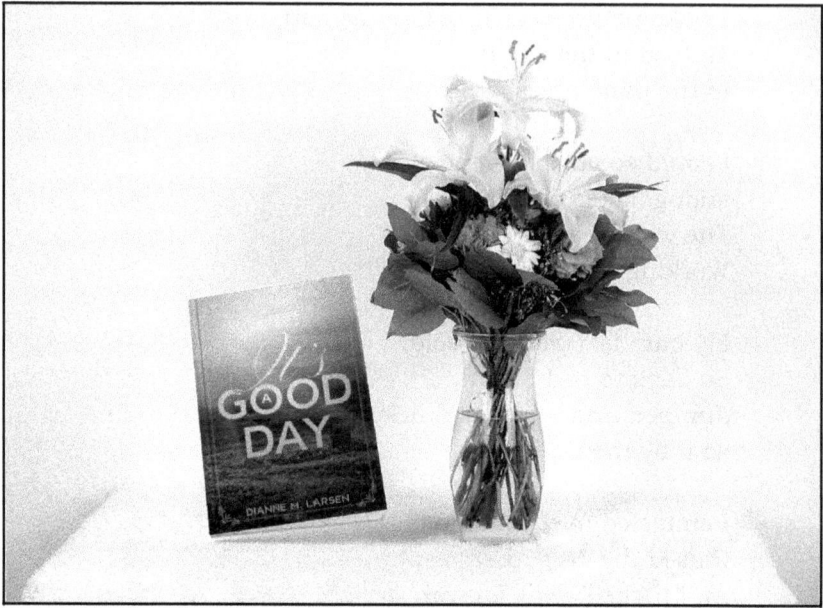

Preface

Several years ago I retired from a job overflowing with contact with other people. If you have retired, you may be familiar with the mixed feelings engendered by your change in routine, social connections, and role in life. Health concerns occupied much of my attention.

My history with the practice of meditation was long and varied. The guidance I received always stressed my need to build a consistent approach. But it wasn't until the universe gave me the gift of cancer that I began meditating in earnest.

Not long after retirement, another development occurred in the form of the COVID Pandemic. Now, not only was I restricted by illness, this deadly disease also isolated me. During this time, I began to receive guidance in my meditation that I should write down what was being said. I did not hear voices. But instead, writing happened spontaneously.

Then I was guided to share the writings on Facebook. This became my new job. Throughout the worst days of the pandemic, it made me think that what had been given to me might be helpful to others. People then suggested that the writings be published, and a good friend, Timothy Banse, at Middle Coast Publishing, stepped forward to further the process.

Finally, I hope these messages and short bursts of communication can be helpful to you. They are meant to be a support to you and the furthering of your daily meditation practice.

Choices

Home is now another world. So much is a world within a world. You are on a course of development that expands your awareness of this. You experience much that comes from limiting your distractions and promoting your inner exploration.

Many in this time have chosen to follow this path. Listen to what they find. They could discover fear or faith, anger or peace. It is a choice you all have. No one is forced into anything. You will see your struggle in making the decision, but it must be made every day in each moment.

There are ways to help the self, such as yoga and meditation. These extend peacefulness; like developing physical muscles, you develop spiritual ones. This enables you to deal with the density of earthly physical existence and the thoughts and emotions that often pass like clouds across your skies.

Find peace these days, and let your skies clear as often as possible. Seek to bring light to others.

- Namaste -

Changing to the New You

Take time to be looking for good. Seek to be as though a child in your looking at the world. Look in wonder, not in judgment. See with fresh eyes all that is here. Be open to being a new person each day as you return from sleep. Every day offers new choices and new ways of being. Being the same each day is not possible even though people try. All of your cells in the body die and are replaced. You also die to the old ways of being to be born each day again. Be at peace with this and affirm that you welcome the new you.

- Namaste -

A Noble Way

Relax at this time. Much is given to explore. Inside you, in times of quiet, you receive much information and support to understand and live your life. There is much to be known and practiced to evolve into the beings you desire.

Living in times of great group challenge is a way to change and know the possibilities you possess. No one is immune from challenge or change, and you proceed in how you decide to deal with it.

Every day you can set your intention in the early hours. Then you practice becoming the person you want to be. Sometimes you will feel successful, and sometimes not. Be kind to yourself as you would a child who is learning to walk. Freeing yourself from judging yourself and others is a noble way to live.

In this time, it is even more of a challenge, as many polarize and form groups of judgment and disfavor.

When you can observe this happening, watch yourself and others. Realization and observation of triggers and reactions is beneficial. All have some triggers. All have some areas to evolve. Be a friend to all, including yourself. Let go of blame, and the misperception of separation for all are truly of the same Source.

- Namaste -

Enriching Your Life

In your time here on earth, you can become a greater expression of the creator. You can become wiser in caring for the self and growing in your relationships with others. You are not required to change others, but you participate in the lives of others through your influence.

You can become a greater expression of the Creator in your time here on earth. You can become wiser in caring for the self as well as growing in your relationships with others. You participate in the lives of others through your influence. It is necessary to drop the burdens the ego develops each day. A build-up of negative thoughts, emotions, and actions clogs your system, and you can become ill or unhappy. Lifting yourself through meditation, yoga, being outside, music, etc., helps to clear yourself of negativity and increase your health.

Even if you still relate daily to the outside world, you can calm and clear how you think, feel and act. If you choose, you will be inspired or guided to find that which enriches you versus that which diminishes you. Choosing to restore yourself through life-giving, healthy means is a sign of evolving your being. Be at peace, seek peace,

- Namaste

Finding the True Self

Do not be dismayed by outward circumstances. Current situations do not last, and all will be different in the future. Those who guide you are with you, and the universe loves you. You are often unaware of this, but you can open your heart to the love there for you.

Many people do not take the time to relax, even for a few moments. For some, this becomes their way of being, to be constantly moving without the inner sensing of themselves and the world beyond the physical. When this happens, life happens to the person, or so it seems.

Awareness of the inner self, the true self, is essential for calm, peace, and happiness. Meditation, which stills the mind and shifts focus, is part of healthy living.

- Namaste -

Seeing the Source in All

Peace in this quiet morning. Clouds do not obscure your sky, and the sun shines about you. Your sight is not dim, and your day stretches before you. Know that all is well with you. Sitting again to start your day, give thanks for all you know, all you are to learn, and all you have to offer.

You are an essential part of all that is. Your presence matters, and you can go forth knowing that you are an active player in the drama of life that unfolds today.

Setting your intentions, you also let go and attract to yourself that which you need to grow. You are here to learn many things and to grow in your ability to care for yourself and others. All are important, all matter, and all are the presence of the Source.

It may be of assistance to sit and visualize first sending love and light to yourself, then sending this out to others in your home, then others in your community, then your state, then your country, and then all over the planet.

You and every being on the planet come from the same Source but come in different flavors of the Source. Recognizing your oneness and uniqueness sets you free to respect each other.

This is a good day to see the Source in each person you meet. Be pleased to meet them and offer them thanks for having entered your life. Trust in the power of awareness and respect. Your peace can spread to others.

- Namaste -

Cultivating Positive Intentions

Now it is warmer, and though you longed for fairer weather, you complain that it is too hot. Instead of complaining, it may benefit you to see the beauty in any weather that comes along. It is not beneficial to think or say negative complaints. To do so is like spreading smoke, so you and those around you experience difficulty seeing and discerning the truth about yourself and your existence.

Again, setting your intentions for being more positive and noticing when you are not are the first steps. Once you see negative thoughts and speech, you can choose what and how you want to think and act.

So often, you are caught in old patterns. Some of these are indeed even shared with others. You can also begin to notice when you share negative patterns, such as saying how horrible the weather is or how awful the world situation is. It is an unconscious choice that many make during their day.

You are encouraged instead to seek to say, think and act in ways that raise you and others around you so that life becomes more affirming and positive. Especially now, with so much fear being generated, an affirming outlook will help. Just as your negativity can ripple out to affect others, so can your positivity.

Regenerate yourself through healthy means just as you would fill your car with gas or charge a battery. Seek out practices that replenish you versus deplete you. Exciting opportunities open as you open yourself to them. Today is a good day to do these things.

- Namaste -

Energy Work

No one is without support, but many don't realize this. Some feel terrible loneliness, but they are not alone. Most people seek to be part of a crowd or group as it makes them feel safer. In truth, all of you are connected and are impacted by others and never not impacting others.

You cannot see radio waves, but they exist, as do microwaves. They both are unseen, but their effects are visible. The same is true of your energy field. Your field of energy is never disconnected from others. Therefore, you are never truly alone.

It helps if one takes the time to sit and become more aware of one's own body. You often ignore the body's feelings and stay stuck in your thoughts. Checking out where your body is stressed and letting go of pain or tension starts with self-awareness.

Your body wants to communicate more to you than you realize. Each day is your opportunity to use the body you have been given to do your chosen work. Taking care of this miraculous body helps you to be successful in your life. Disease often comes when thoughts and emotions negatively impact the body. Calming thoughts and emotions can help balance the body's energy so you can be healthier. Calming thoughts and balancing energy enables you to learn and act on life's lessons.

Today you have an opportunity to sit in silence and listen to what your body tells you. Noticing, asking questions, and accepting the calm you can reach is a good intention. Today is an exciting time to be alive.

- Namaste -

Training Yourself to See

Miracle of a new day! Birds are singing. The sun is shining. A gentle breeze caresses your skin. You are blessed to again be back from sleep to experience the features of life.

Most times, you start the day feeling fresh and new. You awaken and have before you many choices and opportunities. This can be very exciting, yet sometimes daunting or overwhelming. It is as if you have so much to decide and accomplish. How will my path be today? Will it be easy, or will it be difficult? In truth, your path can go many ways and is influenced by how you train yourself to see it.

If you rise and choose worry or fear, your path for the day is much different than if you choose joy and optimism. This is not hard to understand, but many feel that the choice is not theirs and that the world happens to them. In reality, much depends upon your skill in making your own choices.

You can greatly affect how the day how life goes for you by learning skills such as calmness and balance of thoughts and emotions. This is true freedom of choice, and you can begin by establishing a routine for yourself that nurtures and encourages the development of those attributes and skills.

Just as any athlete trains for success in their area or any performer trains to make themselves to be good at their craft, you must set time aside to train to be a happy, calm and healthy person.

It can be exciting to consider in this day how you will go about learning or practicing new or known areas of interest to you. This could include meditation/ prayer, yoga or Tai Chi, walking or sitting in nature, listening to uplifting music, or listening to an uplifting speaker. These and many others wait for you. Today is your class time on earth to learn and grow. Set your intentions and have a blissful day.

- Namaste -

Tuning In

You are here to be happy and assist others in finding their happiness. You cannot direct the happiness of others, but you can do many things that support the enjoyment of others and the world.

Be pleased to see that the road to your purpose is one of the ability to be at peace, calm, and happy. You are not required to live in turmoil or turbulence. It is possible to improve significantly and accept your health and abundance in all areas. You can be freed from feelings of inferiority and feel your beauty and strength. All, regardless of circumstances, can grow towards their joyful living.

You are not here to be as though of sadness or anger. These feelings, these thoughts of lack and fear, are not the true you. You are much more than this. But it is as though many have forgotten their true selves and rush about trying to find something that they miss. Again, if you would but sit with yourself each day and listen to the voice of your true self, you would feel much better and know more about yourself and the world. Just like your TV, if it is not turned on, you can't hear its messages even though the message is being broadcast.

Opening to the messages of life that are true and positive can significantly change and improve your life. It is possible if you do not hold yourself back. Be open to your happiness and your great insight. Develop for yourself the type of affirming routine that brings you joy and fulfillment. You are not meant to live only in fear and pain. Much exists beyond this type of existence. The world can support whatever you choose. It can reflect more pain or anxiety, or it can reflect your joy and light. The choice is yours to make.

Today a good day to practice your skills of cultivating the true you.

- Namaste -

Celebrate Youself Through Silence

Prospering today is totally possible even though much seems in turmoil. Being positive in thought and speech has much to do with your abundance. Saying and thinking negative or dismaying thoughts constantly is a sure way to sink your ship and defeat your desires.

There are layers and layers of yourself to discover. Some feel ashamed, but all are working on some issues, or you would not be here. Perfection is not the goal. Instead, make progress toward your goal. Improvement can be large or small. No one is above this, as everyone is here to learn. Some may be working on forgiveness, others on loving. Change happens constantly, and you may work on several things simultaneously.

Seeking to be aware of yourself and others on a deeper level is a magnificent goal. So often, people rush about seeking material abundance without recognizing how their thoughts and emotions impact their success. It is possible to go your whole life without great insight, so it is a grand celebration when you are brave enough to sit in silence and realize the true you. Today is a good day to be at peace within yourself. You impact the world in marvelous ways as you become more skilled at this. Today is a good day to celebrate your life.

-Namaste -

Setting Sail

Going about your day is a true gift. When you awaken from sleep, you and your body rise to be about this thing you call life. What a gift it is to be awake, to be alive! Each cell of your body is filled with Source energy and fueled by your intentions.

There is today much to be done on many levels. You make plans, but often these plans must change as the day unfolds. Some try very hard to stay on the path they have picked for the day and become upset or overwhelmed when circumstances change, and they cannot stick to what they have envisioned. Others set their intentions to do certain things but can move quickly, skillfully changing or adapting when things do not go as planned.

This ability to adjust is like going sailing. One intends to go out and come back, but in between, the wind blows. One must adjust sails to catch the changes in the breezes so that one can accomplish the goal of sailing. Some are overwhelmed by this. While others view this ability to adapt to the changes as challenging, exciting, and fulfilling. They expect unknown gusts and that they can ride the wind if they pay attention to them.

Each day there is much to adjust to, and often, altering one's course is necessary. Accepting this while setting your intentions is a healthy way to experience your day. Instead of becoming upset over breezes that change your course, you can train yourself to set sail in a new direction. Taking deep breaths when becoming frustrated or disoriented helps to keep yourself upright and able to adjust, perhaps thanking Source for giving you the gift of the gusts that come along and your ability to reset your sails. Even though you may be feeling tossed and turned, skillful use of your consciousness is possible. Set sail today knowing that Source supports you and guides you. That wherever it leads you, there you are.

- Namaste -

The Benefits of Balance

You are fortunate to be in this time. Even though you see much upheaval and strife, there is an opportunity for much growth by all.

Your progress is apparent in how you decide to handle your difficulties. The difficulties are not so much the issue as your decisions on managing them. You can become caught up in the drama being acted out and lose sight of who you truly are as you participate. Or you can become more skillful at recognizing when you have lost your center and balance and take the steps you need to re-center, re-balance and become calm.

The world doesn't need you to be negative, as there is plenty of that. The world needs you to be a being that radiates the universal energy of life, vitality, and serenity. You can see solutions, plan cooperative actions and restore sanity to difficult situations when you are centered. Fear becomes lessened and transformed into clarity and calm. You can interpret things wisely and act accordingly.

So today, perhaps you intend to balance yourself. Take a walk in nature, sing to music or sit in silence and let the true you be present.

- Namaste -

Learning Life Skills

Voices of courage are found everywhere, and voices that express wisdom are often centered on spiritual insight, on knowing themselves and their possibilities. It is evident that many do not take the time to develop that inner sightedness and instead go about with their eyes closed to their truth.

If you would enter that vast space that is part of you, you will find a new perspective that helps you navigate life's storms. Often, most people are not grounded in their inner truth and are tossed about with their emotions and thoughts running wild. It is as if they react to everything and become caught up in chaos. This doesn't have to be your reality. There are skills to learn that keep you focused and calm, even amid chaos. Over time, the cultivation of these skills allows you to be a neutral and discerning influence on the world around you.

All is energy, and so when you change your energy, it changes the energy around you. Perhaps you can attract people and circumstances that benefit you instead of harming you.

Again, it is like any training and development of skill. You start with less, but that is okay because you become more adept as you practice. Not all self-development is without mistakes, but seeing these as necessary steps of a learning process, helps the learner to continue their inner work.

Today is a good day to be open to your growth and supportive of yourself and those around you. Love yourself for your good work and forgive yourself for any mistakes.

- Namaste -

Seeking Freedom

Open your hearts, dear ones, to your freedom. You are a blessed person on this earth, a part of the whole universe. You are not just your body. You are not just your mind. You are not just your emotions. You are a pinpoint of the Source, and as such, you are like the Source.

You have immense potential to express yourself and to be the full potential you possess. Your life is to be spent growing into knowing your true self and manifesting what you can of the divine, the original Source.

There is hope and freedom to be much more than you have been taught. Great peace and calm come for those who can see their true self and potential. This is not within the understanding of many, but more and more have begun to be aware that so much more exists in the world and within themselves.

True freedom is the knowledge and expression of Source. The energy that supplies life to all is manifesting through you and, as such, cares for you. The Source energy illuminates your way and your development. Seek this Source energy and knowledge, for there is perfect freedom.

- Namaste -

Conscious Living

Opening your eyes from sleep, you greet a new day of possibility and choice. Your way is made up of them, and you are here after refreshing yourself to further your education in learning to live.

Nothing impedes you from being the idea you have of yourself. This image of yourself is important as it is the totality of your experience. As you make your way through your day, you do so from this image, and so it is important to consider this idea, this image of yourself.

Honest observation or understanding of this image can assist you in making changes that benefit you. Many people do not take this way and follow a path that is not a very conscious one. Once you begin to see life with the eyes of the observer, you have set in motion the new you.

Today is a good day to set the intention to be aware of yourself. Perhaps you can identify things about yourself, such as your thoughts or emotions. I am nervous. I am happy. Oh, there I was, lost in a particular pattern of thinking. Labeling or identifying helps you to free yourself from unconscious living. Freedom from it is a valuable skill that takes you to a different path of life that begins to help you feel calmer, more peaceful, and more empowered. May you have success in this endeavor.

- Namaste.

The Unfolding Mystery of Each New Day

You are a mystery, and in this time, you seek to understand yourself in more depth. You are an ever-growing and evolving being. You are not static, so there are new things to notice about yourself every day. It is not known, therefore, with absolute certainty, what you will do or how you will act with others. You have tendencies, but you are also a fluid form of energy that seeks its way toward greater skills and knowledge.

Today is a good day to celebrate the new person you woke up to become. Putting lack of skills and mistakes from previous days behind you sets you free to move ahead into newly charted water. You can set intentions for the day and observe how things progress. Give thanks for being aware and awake.

- Namaste -

The Gardener

Growing your vegetables or fruits is a healthy endeavor. It is one of beginning to take charge of your health. It is also for you an opportunity to interact with nature on a profound level. You interact with many elements such as the soil, light, weather, and other creatures. You are also outside, where the atmosphere is different. You then can take into your body the embodiment of your work and your connection to nature.

There are many ways to become more aware, to grow yourself as you would, in a sense, grow your fruits and vegetables. You can set your intention to become a greater conscious being and plant the seed for your growth. You can cultivate the area around you so that you can grow each day.

You know that it is challenging to grow in darkness, so each day, you can seek to bring light into your life. How do you bring life-giving light into your life? There are many ways that can be accessed. Perhaps you can pray/meditate, walk in nature, sing favorite songs, and practice Yoga/Qigong. Maybe you wish to be creative by making something new that delights your heart.

Growing yourself is a task that goes better as you realize what you are doing and give it a priority each day, not making it drudgery but a clear and joyous choice.

In this day, may you grow yourself within yourself. May your growth positively support you and those around you.

- Namaste -

Awakening

So many times, you are distracted by things such as your individual and group fears. These fears are often not well founded in the reality of the situation. Your mind obsesses, developing a story about this fear, distracting you from the truth, the possibilities that could be present for you.

It is important to start catching those times when contemplating negative thoughts. Once you identify or notice this, you can begin to replace them with a more positive reality, choosing your thoughts, and making them ones that serve you better.

No one is above the process of learning to use this skill. All must wake from unconscious living to become better at creating a higher consciousness. Do not criticize yourself for going into the mind's negative, fearful stories. Instead, love yourself as though hugging yourself each time you become aware of what you have been doing. Being grateful for waking up to living in peace and love is a good thing. Without the negative story building, you would not recognize its absence.

Today is a good day to set your intention to train yourself in developing and using this skill. Love yourself, whether it is difficult or easy.

- Namaste -

Knowing Yourself

Observe yourself, and you will learn much that is useful to you. How is it that you think, feel and act? Can you become better at knowing yourself in these ways? If you become more adept at observing yourself, you can become more skillful at accepting yourself as you are.

You are not a stagnant point but an ever-changing and evolving being. Like the universe, you exist in and it in you, you become different each moment. No one stays the same.

Consider yourself throughout the different growth changes or stages of your life. Be loving, observant, and accepting of yourself. Do you judge a plant as it grows from a seed? Do you judge an egg as it hatches into a baby bird? Yet so often, that is what you do to yourselves and others.

Today you can set your intention to observe change and growth in yourself and others. Training yourself to observe rather than judge is helpful for your happiness and equanimity. Your doing so helps the world.

- Namaste -

Balancing Your Energy

In this world, there is much busyness, much going on around you. There are many, many distractions and opportunities that come to you. It is essential that you transmit out to the world the energy that you want and that you attract to you the energy that you want. All of this is like the ebb and flow of energies.

It is very important to balance yourself and your energy in mind, body, and emotions as often as possible. This keeps things flowing smoothly and helps you become the wiser, more evolved being you seek to be.

Your experience depends mainly on how you set yourself up. In placing importance on balancing yourself, you take in and give out the energy that is more suited to being happy and freer of concerns.

Sometimes you have negative energy going on, and you can tell that it is happening. It is then beneficial to change that energy by healthy means. What works in this way for you? Excessive eating, drinking, and many other paths are not what balances you.

Today it would be beneficial to notice how your energy is. When it is not what you want it to be, your intention can be to change it by finding new means or by using healthy means that you already know work for you.

It is also beneficial to give thanks for the opportunities or challenges that come your way, as many are there to help you grow in awareness and support your evolution. Give thanks, balance yourself and love yourself for your ability to see the truth.

- Namaste -

Peeling Away Layers

Sorrow sometimes comes your way when you realize that you have peeled away another layer for you to see into yourself and discover the errors you have made without being aware of it. Seeing that you have been doing things or living unconsciously can be uncomfortable.

Again, you can become a more skillful person here as you express thanks and gratitude for becoming more aware of how to live and be more proficient. This position has given you the first step in becoming able to change and grow. See this awareness as a gift to you. You can be freer to live as you become more aware of negative patterns of thought, feeling, and action.

There are always more layers to peel away so you can evolve. Again, you don't need to judge yourself harshly. But instead, you can choose to be more compassionate and kind to yourself.

Congratulate yourself on seeing a higher truth. Sit with your realizations and ask for clarity and guidance on how to change the old patterns. The vibration you send out to the Source will send or give you the assistance and clarity you seek.

Today, look for guidance in each step you take. Accept the love and help that comes your way. -

- Namaste -

Listening to the World

As you become more open to knowledge about yourself and the universe, you begin to see that you are an intricately involved being with many layers of consciousness and connections with the rest of the world.

Often people are self-isolated in their little world of consciousness, and they don't feel or see that they are truly a part of the vastness of being. There is much more than just your own thoughts, feelings, and actions. There is much more to this world of energy and connections.

It is beneficial to wake more and more to this reality and train yourself to be more aware. Much more knowledge is available. Much more is still to be explored and experienced. It is as though you begin to awaken from sleep, and you open your eyes to see the world around and within. Acceptance that there is more than just your being and your interpretation of things leads you to want to listen to the world and understand more about it and the being you call you.

Today is an excellent day to periodically recognize this connection, rise out of your routine to notice nature or the room you are in, truly listen to another, and sit in silence and explore within. Letting yourself have these periods of awareness is a blessing.

- Namaste -

Endless Being

You are on a journey that has no end. You are going through the passing of time, but time has no end. You have no end in the sense that a continuous flow of energy is part of you.

Never are you alone as there is no break in the energy that is between all things. You will not be alone, even though your ability to sense this may be limited. As you age, your time as a specific being may come to an end, but the true you, your life energy, does not die. The energy that is this being you call you is not limited to this life. You cannot die if you are a part of this energy. You will change and not continue as the current pinpoint of energy.

This knowledge can bring you peace of mind as you know that your spirit will soar while your body falls away. Time here is a flexible thing and varies in speed and perception. Your time needs to be wisely spent to gain the maximum benefit. You are here merely to grow in knowing and gaining the skills for doing so. Today is a good day to grow in your awareness.

- Namaste -

Opening the Heart

Opening up your heart is the best thing you can do in these days of disquiet and hunger for love. Many people have learned to close their hearts because of fear, much like a flower closes its petals when the light grows dimmer. Closing your heart may feel like the safest, wisest thing to do, but it causes many problems. A closed heart cannot take in or give out the loving energy essential for health. A closed heart does not allow a person to love or be loved as they need, but it shuts down nourishment from the Source. Becoming more open-hearted is a task for all to pay attention to.

This is a start if you can set aside even a small amount of time each day to be by yourself. Another step is to sit in silence and allow the heart to become more aware and open to the needed energy. You can do this alone or with others of like intention.

This is not the only way to open your heart, but if done daily, the heart begins to open, and the receiving and giving of heart energy grows in strength. As you do this daily, you begin to feel the benefits in your thoughts, emotions, and actions. Your joy increases along with your insight and peace. Today is a good day to set the intention to set aside time to be alone, to focus on the inner you.

- Namaste -

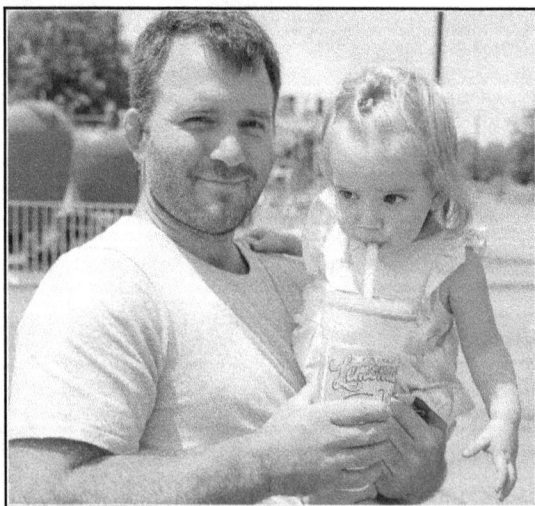

Developing the Skill of Kindness

Kindness is a very important topic for these days. Kindness is potentially the concept that needs to be examined so that more of it can be expressed in your life and the world. Kindness comes from feelings of understanding and compassion. To reach this stage, one must decrease fear and angry types of emotions. If one can gain a more calm and peaceful state, it is more possible to reach the kindness you can and need to express towards yourself and others.

For this to occur, one can cultivate true kindness. It again is a part of a skill set. Some have developed greater skills in this area, but all are able to do so, especially if that is your intention. All can benefit from developing the attributes of calm, peace, gratitude, and kindness. It is not that you don't have these things. It is that often you have forgotten or not developed them well. It is like someone who wants to run in a race. Usually, one must practice and build their bodies to increase their speed and endurance. It isn't that the person is bad because they lack speed and endurance. They just need to develop this part of themselves to accomplish their goal.

Like the racer, you can develop yourself so that you can live with more success in being kind to yourself and others. Think of holding a new baby or young child. Feel how easy it is to be kind to them, speak words of kindness, and open your heart to loving them. If you are able to go there, you can see how to begin your skills. So often, you judge yourself and others as unworthy of kindness. This is not the truth. All need and desire kindness.

Today is a good day to set your intention to give kindness to yourself and the world around you. Start to cultivate this attitude. Notice when you are triggered to be less than kind and reset yourself. Let it go and try again.

- Namaste -

A Wider View

Seeing clearly is not just a physical function. Your eyes aren't the only part of you that has sight. When you close your eyes, you can still see many scenes in your mind. Often people limit this ability by choosing only to see things from a limited perspective. This entails only choosing the sight that comes with the conditioning or culture you have been immersed in. This leads you to go through life with blinders and only value things as you have been taught. This leads to many misinterpretations or mistakes that limit your life.

If you can set about opening your eyes as it were to other ways of seeing the world, you would increase your wisdom and your ability to be at home in many more worlds. You will be able to be kinder as you will understand others better.

Seeing a more expansive view asks for you to be open, accept things from different perspectives, and put yourself in the shoes of others, whether human or animal. How does this one see the world? This is a challenge for many, as this may conflict at some level with how the viewer has been taught to see the world. But does this have to be so?

Letting go of limited sight is another skill that can be learned and needs to be developed for the people on this earth to be able to succeed. It is possible for many who see beyond limited appearances to affect the entire planet as this momentum grows.

Seek today to see others in a different more understanding, compassionate way. Seek to see yourself more compassionately.

- Namaste -

Ripples of Peace

It seems to many that there is no order in these days. Many are living in fear and do not know what is to come. Because of this inner and outer chaos, it is very important to balance yourself for your own good and the good of the world around you.

You may consider that you can do nothing to help the situation, but this is an error. Your contribution is like throwing a stone into a pond in that the effect is to send ripples out that impact the shore. You are an essential being for helping the world to change.

Then comes the question, do you want peace and calm, or are you stuck in drama? Can you conceive of or visualize a world where change is present but where there is more insight, freedom of choice, and openness towards others? Now is a time to consider a different manner of building up the daily and universal life on earth.

It is not impossible to do this, but again it is a skill that needs to be developed. When learning to ride a bike, it seems almost impossible until you reach the stage when you are balanced enough to suddenly glide along in freedom of movement.

Consider yourself today as a change agent for peace and love. Why not? You are empowered by your life force and connected to all. Seek to grow in awareness and skill. Seek to change the world from your growing sense of peace and calm.

- Namaste.

Your Best Friend

Suppose you were to look at yourself and the world around you differently. Suppose that instead of seeing only with your physical eyes, you also saw with your heart, your intuition.

Many times you are stuck in looking at things in such a way as to hide the true essence of things, and so you are unable to make sense of why you are here and how to learn the tasks you have chosen to accomplish.

What can you do about this dilemma? This is a starting point when you ask this question and when you are tired of looking at the world through the same eyes, instead desiring to see things differently, perhaps wiser, perhaps happier.

It is alright to admit that you have had deficits in seeing things, but this is only a step. Some get stuck here, but that is only a step, not your totality. You are much more than your deficits, and it helps to begin to be kinder and more compassionate to yourself. Would you constantly criticize an earnest young child for the normal developmental stages it must go through? No, because that would not help them to grow, change for the best and develop their potential. Instead, you would seek to give them encouragement, positive support, and caring.

This is the first step in seeing the world with different eyes. Make it your intention to be your own best friend. Say positive, uplifting things to yourself. Encourage yourself to grow and change. Be a support to yourself. Much can be accomplished through exploring the inner you. Sitting in silence and developing the eyes of inner sight will also be of value.

True sighted-ness is yours if you desire it. Seeing yourself and the world through loving, compassionate eyes is within your grasp.

- Namaste.

Cultivating Life

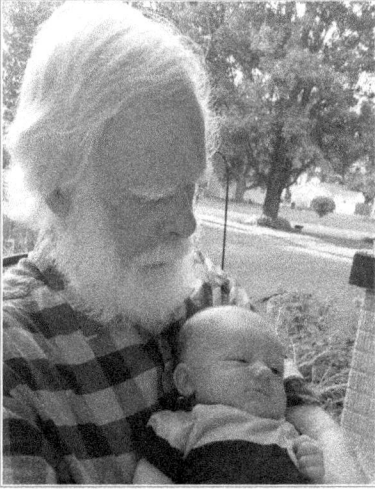

All of life is energy from the Source. Life is energy that illuminates your body and allows you to be present in this time. Without the life energy present in your body, you cannot live. It is important to honor and be aware of this vital energy to more effectively manage it. Learning more about your energy is another step in the skill of life. Teaching others, especially children, is so helpful.

Sitting in silence is one way to be more aware of your unique way of expressing the energy of Source. As you become more aware of this precious sustaining force, you can heal yourself on many different levels and keep your health and vitality. You can help others to heal and learn to manage their energy.

Today, notice your energy. Replenish when you can through healthy means. Express your gratefulness as often as you can remember to.

- Namaste -

Breathing Into Life

Surprise is a common reaction to unanticipated events that occur in your life. You often see the day as another routine you have done before, repeating your schedule and tasks repeatedly. Then comes a new occurrence that upsets your common routine and you are startled by it, perhaps feeling happy or displeased. In any event, all experience this change at times. Sometimes you handle it with ease and other times not. Change can be mild or like an earthquake that shakes and rattles you to your core. When you are greatly disturbed by events, what can you do to help right yourself and attain balance again?

Many will take this event and use it to become more skilled, more aware. Some will, when they can, thank the event for helping them to change, to see things from a better perspective, but that may take some time to get to. In the immediate time of your surprise, it is helpful to realize that you are reacting and to focus on your breath, which most likely has become rapid and shallow. It is beneficial to change to a slower, deeper breath so that your body and mind can become calmer and better able to process the event. You cannot be disturbed and calm at the same time, so choosing to calm yourself will be of help to you.

Today is a good day to practice slow and deep breathing. It is a skill all can develop. Take time throughout your day to focus on your breath, even if only for a short time. Breathe into your abdomen through your nose and let yourself exhale through your mouth. Do this slowly at least three times so that you slow down your body and mind. Give thanks for being able to breathe and the opportunity to focus on it.

- Namaste -

More to it Than You Thought

You begin to see that there is so much more to things than you thought or were taught. The person that is you is a much more complex being than your first understanding. So much time is spent learning to master your body and its functions, such as walking, eating, et cetera. Then you must learn how to behave and learn to share and live without physical violence towards others. Then you are asked to master the language, customs, and culture. Yet often, you are not taught spiritual concepts other than those of control and behavior.

There is much more to you, your connections, and your relationship to the universe. When you look at the night sky, you see much that is amazing. There are so many stars there for so many worlds. When you consider your body and the number of cells that all function together to keep your body working, you again can be amazed. Physics teaches you that there is even more to reality, that energy can be distilled down to math concepts, and that energy supports all creation.

You begin to understand that there is so much more going on than you have understood and that there is much more to learn, that learning and changing, growing and evolving never stops. All creation is spinning and changing, and you are a part of it. Such a perspective changes your outlook on life and the world you spin in.

Today open yourself to learning more. Observe what you can about yourself and others around you. How are you interacting? How are you connected? How can you help each other to see and understand your connections? Your life is not an experience of loneliness but rather a connectedness to all.

- Namaste -

Never Alone

Precious is life to all who are conscious of themselves. Being grateful teaches you to see the uniqueness of many things, including the presence of others in your life. Sensing the beauty and connection with other people and nature is the work you were sent here to do.

You are never alone because of these connections. You may appear, through limited sight, to be alone, but you cannot truly be alone due to you all being connected through Source energy. You may feel alone or lonely, but in truth, you are all a part of each other.

Feeling and knowing this connection is again a skill you can strengthen. Sending positive intentions to all you meet today will be good practice of this skill of conscious connection. With each person or animal you meet, send or wish for them that they experience joy, be healthy and happy, and grow or progress. Even those who you have negative energy with need these things. As you grow your compassion for others, your own energy changes and becomes more positive.

So today, set your intention to increase your skill to connect with others. Set your intention to practice compassion for all who have feelings too. Forgive yourself when you forget, and be grateful when you remember to be kind.

- Namaste -

Starting the Day

As you greet this new day, you welcome new experiences that help you understand yourself and the world in ways you may not have anticipated. Leaving open the gate to your heart enables you to walk into the day without fear or concern about the future or regrets about the past.

You are who you are at this minute. You are free to experience life as it comes to you. Shaking off impediments to your experience is helpful for your evolution. Lacking fear or anxiety helps you become more loving and happier.

It is of benefit then to set yourself up to go about your day from a balanced starting point. Setting your intention to be balanced in your steps for the day is like spreading out your energy in a calm pool of clear water. It helps you to be able to see more clearly what is around you and allows you to make clearer decisions. The more you practice this start to each day, the more skillful you become.

Today is a good day to sit, stand or lie down in the calmness of your inner self. Stay there for a time, whether short or long and cultivate your growth of peace. Then rise and take with you that peace into the new day. If storms beset you, come back to yourself, accept and love yourself and go out again.

- Namaste.-

Feeling Connected

What an awesome day is this one. You are back in your body after your sleep and you are ready to begin again.

No where is there anyone just like you and no day is going to be anything the same as it has been. Even though you adhere to a routine, you cannot be the same. You are ever changing, growing, evolving, becoming. If you were afraid of something yesterday, your perspective has changed with rising of the sun and the rising of your consciousness in your body. No one is here to block your growth. They may have agreed to be your teacher, but they, in a sense, have agreed to help you along your way.

If you can grasp that all are connected, then you begin to see that all affect each other. All of you touch each other in some way, taking and giving breath to each other's reality.

Today set your intention to feel more deeply the energy exchange between all beings. Sense here, on a deeper level, where you set your focus and you will be more aware. You will be more at home as you recognize this community of being.

- Namaste -

Set the Tone

Going into your day, you awaken from sleep and begin to gather yourself for your work. You may move about in this new day by opening your eyes. You may seek to be prepared for the coming of dawn and your new day. Perhaps there is a tendency to fulfill your routine without much notice of what is happening. You may fumble through your preparation without much awareness of your potential for the day.

Gathering your energy at the beginning is more advantageous rather than wandering about in a daze. Gathering your energy helps you to have a better start to your day, and you will feel better physically and spiritually.

If you can, sit in silence. Let yourself start to set the tone for the day by being grateful for whatever comes to your mind. Being grateful opens your mind to the positive energy that you need to fuel yourself for your day. Too much-scattered energy doesn't get you as far.

So this morning, begin by closing your eyes and saying to yourself, "I am grateful for . . ." Do this for as long as you are able. Even a short time is beneficial. Take the time you can and notice how much better you feel as you prepare for your day.

- Namaste -

Remembering Who You Are

You are a blessed creation of the energy of the Source, and you are the universe's energy. Much about you is not known or remembered so you can become confused. It is part of your work to discover or remember who you truly are. Connecting your mind, emotions, body, and spirit to the reality of who you are is essential.

Being a creation of Source energy gives you the fantastic opportunity to be alive in this time. You can become aware of this potential, and you become so much more when you do. It isn't necessary to be correct, but it is good to be aware, observe, and realize your part in the creation around you.

Believing in yourself and exploring yourself is the adventure of your life. Discovering, understanding, and feeling your connection to all of the rest of creation is your blessing. Nowhere is there not the principle of oneness. Diversity is the unique expression of Source, but all is still Source energy.

There are so many levels of Source energy as to be infinite. You don't need to understand it all, but you can be aware of your connections. Great joy comes from appreciating the energy that makes up you and the rest of the universe. Today you can become more of the observer. Set your focus on noticing what you think, feel, and do. Notice this in others, in nature. Express your gratefulness.

- Namaste -

Make It Better

When you start your day, you have a blank page on which you can create a new story. See yourself sitting with this blank page before you. What do you want to put on this particular page? The choices are infinite. You can write or draw and make for yourself the kind of story that pleases you. Will it be an adventure, a drama, or perhaps a comedy? Maybe it will be some of all woven into your day.

At times the number of choices you have may seem overwhelming, and you wonder where to start or how to sustain the effort to make so many choices. At other times, you feel excited to be so free. Then there may be days when your page seems like an unending list of things that feel imposed on you.

Know that you can improve your day by being centered on yourself. You can become centered at any time during your day, but it helps to start that way. Then take what breaks you can throughout your day to re-center and remember that things are good, that you are okay, and that you have a choice regarding how you think, feel and move.

So this morning, before you start your day, breathe deeply, perhaps closing your eyes. State to yourself what you are grateful for and set your intentions for the day. Not a list of have-to's, but what or how you desire to be, think, or feel. Send loving thoughts to yourself and others. Vision yourself walking in confidence, kindness, and safety along the path you create. Know that your intentions help to set the tone for all that happens.

- Namaste -

Ripples in a Pond

There is a great need for those who can shine or reflect light to the world and others. It is the time to be as centered and aware as you can be to help raise the vibration of all around you. You may think that you have no influence on the world, but in reality, since all are connected, you have a significant effect on the whole. because there is much darkness in your world at present, it is important to reflect to others the lightness of loving kindness so that it spreads out from you like ripples in a pond, touching everyone it reaches. Don't doubt your worth, value, or the importance to the reality being created in each moment. You can choose to be a loving light reflection and influence not only your health but also the world's health.

To be this reflection, you must clear out fear and worry and know there is more than discord. To do this, you must balance yourself by centering yourself. You can use many different approaches to centering. Meditation, being in nature, singing, and being creative are just a few examples. Finding and cultivating these things that bring you calm, joy or peace is important for you and the world around you.

Today is a good day to nurture the energy of the universe within and around you. Know that you matter and how you choose to live matters.

- Namaste -

Is That All There Is?

Your life is a variety of experiences. Since you were first born, you have looked curiously at life and its complexities. Your eyes have looked outward for directions in maps, plans, books, etc, or, looking outward is not the sum total of your life but your reality.

Looking only outward can provide endless stimulation but is not endlessly satisfying. You can experience many things, but after a while, something may seem to be missing. Only so much food, drink, vacations, events, and books can be enjoyed. And you may feel that this cannot be all there is to your life. Perhaps you feel disturbed by this feeling, these thoughts. "I have all of these things, these experiences, but still I am not satisfied?" You may be upset with yourself and wonder, " What is wrong with me?"

This is a positive step in your life, not a negative one. This dissatisfaction with the physical limitations of your life can lead you to desire more. This can lead you to question things, but this is not bad. This questioning and dissatisfaction can lead to your growth, to your exploring new ways to look at your life and world. Change can be uncomfortable but embraced and viewed as another opportunity to evolve, grow, and mature.

Today is a good day to look at yourself, express gratitude for what you see, and open your heart to experience, learn, and grow yourself past what you have been before. Accept your ability to question, seek, to evolve as a good thing in your life. Be at peace with moving forward.

- Namaste -

A Gift for the World

Sitting in the morning sun's light, you greet your new day of adventure and growth. Like the plant that adds fresh leaves and petals, you will add knowledge to yourself today.

Freedom is a curious thing. You both crave and fear it at times. With freedom comes the ability to choose and the responsibility to choose as wisely as possible.

Setting the start to your day, you have endless potential for exploring and discovering. You can truly be inspired and put the energy from inspiration into action. Your day is a tiny bit of your life, yet it is very important to develop into the person you desire to be.

When you list the qualities of who you want to be, you support it becoming a reality. Saying to yourself things such as I am strong, I am kind, I am wise, and so on, sets into your vibration those concepts about your being. It is essential to do so daily to shift from negative self-concepts to positive ones. Just as you would speak kind and loving statements to a child, you need to say them to yourself.

Being present and positive are great gifts you give yourself and, therefore, the world. As you lift your vibration, you raise the vibration of the world. Because all are connected, you do your part to better yourself and the energy of others.

Today is a good day to increase your positive charge and help charge up the world around you. Become a part of the universal store of love.

- Namaste -

Knowing the Truth

Progress is knowing that you are perfect in all ways, knowing deep in your heart that you are worthy even when you are growing, and making choices that are less than perfect. Your true self knows this truth about you, and when you go to that state of understanding, you can look at yourself with compassion and love.

Nowhere is there, not Source energy. This energy that science has identified is the building block for you and all other things. You are all made of the same stuff but are made into individualized points of energy. Knowing that all are made from the same energy and material can help diminish the sense of aloneness or alienation many feel.

When you sit in silence, you can experience the reality of peace and acceptance. Wouldn't you rather be at peace and feel acceptance and love for yourself and others than fear, upset, and anger? When you feel upset, it is your message to reset yourself. When you are in balance, all makes sense. All is love.

Today is a good day to be in this state of balance as much as possible. You can seek healthy ways to be in harmony and know the truth about yourself and your world.

- Namaste -

Flex Your Muscles

You are a complex being, a person with many layers of energy and many stages of development. Looking back at pictures of your life, you can see how you have grown and changed. Isn't it wonderful that you have been able to do this, that you have been able to change, grow and mature into the person you are today?

All people change and continuously grow in their ability to manifest more of their potential. No one is without this capacity to be more aware and more accomplished. All are where they should be at this particular moment. All are doing their best to be enlightened. All are moving towards their fulfillment.

Thinking positively about yourself and others is easy, and it gets easier as you cultivate this skill. Doing this changes your perception of the world and gives you much peace and calm. One way to help yourself see yourself positively is to practice the art of being grateful. Being grateful changes any negative into a positive. Today is a good day to sit, stand, lie down, or walk while you express to yourself anything that comes to mind. Say to yourself, I am grateful for . . .

Doing this upon rising, several times during the day, and before going to sleep will help you to reset your thoughts, emotions, and actions. The positivity you manifest will help you and others around you.

Today is a good day to practice this skill. Whenever you feel down, angry or out of balance in some way, use this skill. Flex your gratitude muscles and become stronger in balancing your thoughts and emotions.

- Namaste -

Reset and Rebalance

Open wide your heart and mind today. Let the light of health, happiness, and love permeate all the cells of your wonderful body. You are a radiant being, a soul expressing itself through your body, mind, emotions, and spirit.

No one else in this life is the same as you, yet you are all of one creation, spirit, and source of energy. Even the stars and their galaxies are of the same substance. You and the birds and trees share this makeup. All are connected.

Sometimes this feels real to you, and at other times your energy condenses, and you feel alone, jealous, angry, sad, or confused. These times come and go like the weather. Some days are sunny, and you are able to see your reality much better, with more clarity. Other days are dark and stormy, and you lose your balance while you walk your path.

There is no value in condemning yourself for this. It would be better to acknowledge the storms when they pass and hug yourself when you can. Speak words of loving kindness to yourself. Know that this is a part of life; as you grow, you become aware more rapidly, and the storms become less intense and shorter in duration.

Today, take time, even if short, to be kind to yourself. Nurture yourself in healthy ways. Affirm that you are calm, happy, loving, etc. Saying these kinds of statements to yourself helps to reset, rebalance your walking on your path. Seek out sources of positivity and light. Peace be within and about you.

- Namaste -

Growing the Knowing

The promise of the new day is becoming conscious of more that surrounds you, enfolds you, and is you. This is a promise that you will grow in ways that perhaps surprise you. Nowhere is there not a promise of growth, of becoming more than you were just a moment ago. How do you measure this moment? Is it the blink of an eye? Is it a second? Is it eternity, or is it here and gone?

You have been given the power to make choices, to go beyond being of animal nature. You can be more and more conscious, but this takes you along the path of becoming aware of things that go beyond the teachings that you grew up with, the perspective that you have grown comfortable with, and the reality of the past.

When you take steps to be more aware and wiser, you agree to look with new eyes at yourself and the life you are immersed in. You will not and cannot be the same as you were a minute ago. So, why not grow in ways that serve, that help others to open their eyes also?

You are not alone, never have been, never will be. You are part of all that is. How can you not be continually surprised as you go from the known into further known?

It is okay to wake up and be different. So many try not to, but it is futile. When you encounter this in yourself, be kind, be of service, and be as gentle and loving as you would be to a newly born baby. You are being newly reborn all along your path.

- Namaste -

Create Your Reality

Upon this spinning planet, you are living. Day turns to night and night to day. In reality, your life span is short, but not without the time needed to learn to be aware and conscious. You are not trapped by circumstance in that you are able to choose to decide many things for yourself.

Because your thoughts influence your emotions and actions, it is very important to learn to guide your thoughts to be healthy. Then you can create the life you desire.

Most desire a life of happiness and health. These desires are possible if you become more adept at governing your thoughts. As you think, you are.

If you constantly devalue yourself and entertain thoughts of disaster or drama, that is what you will manifest in your life. The universe will respond by promoting the energy you gather and emit.

So if you intend to help yourself live a more rewarding life, learn and practice the skills of positive thinking and positive self-talk. Cultivate this discipline, not to deny reality but to create it.

Today is a good day to be grateful and generate as much positivity as possible.

- Namaste -

With New Eyes

There is more for you than the now. You are driven to explore all that is given to you, so you are curious about many things. Perhaps you are curious about love, maybe freedom, perhaps happiness. You then seek many experiences that reflect the opportunities to study these things. So many of your life experiences are solely to help you grow in the chosen areas. While they may seem random, they are gifts you have attracted to yourself to help you learn what is important to you.

It is if the benefit to ask then, "What am I to learn from this?" Stepping back to ask the question helps you to see what is going on more clearly. You are always a part of the challenge and its resolution. Observing rather than reacting is a valuable tool for solving a challenge or changing the outcome.

Today is a good day to set the intention to look at the situations in your life with new eyes and understanding. Be aware that you are doing this. The answers may come quickly or not until another time, but if you ask for clarity and understanding, it will be answered. Another tool, again, is learning to sit in silence, ask your questions and listen for the answers, the knowledge that comes from your most profound understanding, your true self.

- Namaste -

Your Cosmic Curriculum

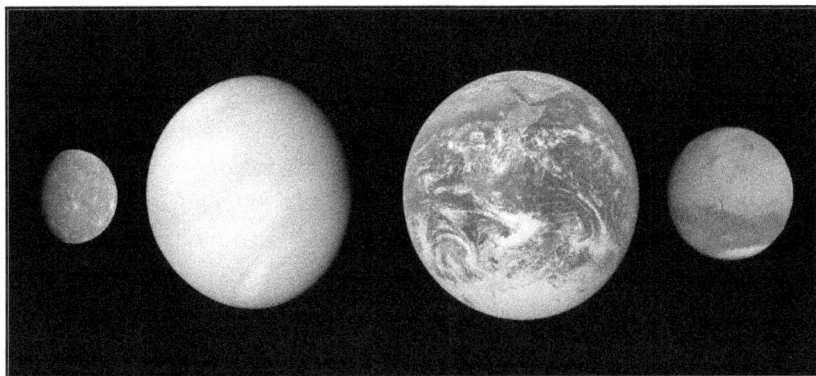

Be prepared today to go to life's school, not in the physical sense, but in the sense of learning how to live your life better. Every day you wake, you come back from Source to further your growth through life lessons. Perhaps you have chosen to learn how to love yourself and others. Maybe you have selected the subject of helping those around you heal from sadness. Perhaps you have chosen to study how to communicate with others through writing or music. So many different topics are available to you.

To be prepared to study, it helps to know that this is your mission and that you have chosen to explore the different topics in your life. Life is not just random occurrences. But instead, it is a cosmic curriculum that assists you in evolving and becoming a more aware, awake, and action-oriented being.

Today, ask yourself what you are working on. Be inspired by the course you have chosen. Set your intention to be at peace in the classroom you call life.

- Namaste -

Where Did That Come From?

You are given many opportunities each day. These opportunities are there for you to decide on which to choose and use. No one decides this but yourself for yourself. Everyone has this dynamic in their life. Sometimes groups of people combine their choices, which can yield more energy power.

Many things influence your choices, so the wise person looks to see what these influences might be. Many times the answers are started in the past and continue today. Small children often are influenced by the choices of others, and the reaction of the child is forgotten. The source of the reaction is buried deeply but continues its influence on choices as the child grows, so that often by the time the child is an adult, the response becomes very strong. This can lead to actions or reactions that spring from an unconscious or an unrecognized source. This may lead to the closing of the heart or mind to many opportunities that come to the person.

It is helpful then to observe how you react to things. If there is a pattern, you will be able, with practice, to identify the pattern. As you mature, you have much information about yourself and can begin to examine your patterns and choices, not to judge or condemn, but in compassion to help to heal and change so that your being is happier and your path easier.

Sitting in silence and asking for help with this will bring you answers and fresh ways to think, feel and act. Your true self knows the answers to your questions and is your best source for caring and objective information. When the truth comes through to you, it is a KNOWING that is without a doubt.

So today, set your intention. Perhaps it is to continue or start this sitting in silence with yourself, listening for the wisdom you naturally possess. Be at peace, even if for a short time.

- Namaste -

Being a Light Worker

Immense change comes to you in days to follow. You will feel very different in the days that come. Your own thoughts and feelings will be challenged as you are called upon to become more filled with light and hope for the future. You have asked for there to be these changes in order to learn and grow. Past concepts are being challenged as you need to be challenged to rearrange your path.

Nowhere is there more than what you can handle, but now is the time to spread calm, peace, generosity, and positivity. In order to do this, you must nurture it within yourself first. When called upon, you must remind yourself not to spread fear but instead to encourage yourself and others with images of loving-kindness.

A word to yourself and others here and there is of great importance for encouraging needed changes. Be supportive of yourself and others. Carve out time to nurture yourself so that you can be of service and that you are grounded in Source energy. Recognizing this Source of energy is vital for life and fulfilling your purpose.

Practice being employed as a light worker. Keep an open mind and nurture the positive, not the dark. Speak words of illumination, not condemnation. Be the person that is hopeful and certain that all will be well.

- Namaste -

Basic Universal Law

This is a day of great joy with the potential for much happiness in your life and your world. There is much to be celebrated as you were able to awaken this day and go about your life.

Your body draws breath and takes you where you need or want to go. Your mind is able to grasp new thoughts, and your heart feels new feelings. You are blessed to be alive and able to communicate with others. Perhaps you are able to do some things that make your spirits soar. Perhaps you are able to help others who you love or maybe others you don't know. Are you able to do the work you have chosen for today? Are you able to have moments of quiet here and there?

Yes, it is a day filled with blessings. A day to give thanks for. To your benefit, you approach this new day with gratitude, for the more you dwell on the positive, the more positives you create for yourself. It is a fundamental law of the universe that what you sow, so shall you reap. Being positive sets the stage for the drama you call life to be aligned with the energy of light and love.

When thoughts of darkness trouble you, it is within your power to notice what you are creating and then choose a different way to think. All is not lost if you have angry or bitter thoughts, so be kind to yourself. Be understanding of your fears, and like a good friend, help yourself move into a more loving expression. Today is a good day to set the intention to be joyous and grateful.

- Namaste -

The Common Thread

Every day you awaken as a new person, a new you. Your being comes back refreshed to begin a new day. You are like the baby that awakens from sleep and sees the world with fresh eyes.

Today is the sum total of all of your days so far in this life. It is not that you are without a past or future, but that who you are now is a new person. In fact, you are new and growing in every moment of every day. It is as though you have been developing for this unique moment and a new moment continues to pop up. Endless new moments come along, and you cannot go back to the being you were even at the start of reading this.

You constantly evolve and change so that you are able to become and keep becoming. It is possible to develop into a very different you than you were in the early stages of this lifetime. As you grow and change, you reflect much to the world in the light that is you. Your self is much more than just your experience, and you are not caught in being the same person, same attitudes, or same perspectives.

You are a tiny amount of the universe. You are a reflection of the whole, even though you are just a part. In all beings is this phenomenon of the whole reflected in part. All are connected by the simple nature of being the same energy, the exact reflection. You are not alone. You are never separate. You can't be disconnected from the rest of creation.

How does this common thread affect you and the other beings around you? Can you, at times, glimpse this commonality? If you intend to see it today, affirm it and focus on seeing the connections you have to all there is. Instead of focusing on difference, focus on similarities and common essence. See that which is alike versus that which is different.

- Namaste -

Light Grows

These days many things seem strange to you. There are energies that appear to be pulling you this way and that so that you wonder what is the best path, the safest one for you to take? So for many, these times are trying and disquieting. It is as though you are standing at the ocean's edge, wondering what to do next. Do I wade in? Do I swim? Do I turn around and walk the other way? How do I or should I react to what is happening around me?

It is suggested that you comfort yourself in this time, not by addictive or harmful behaviors, but by developing the ability to help yourself feel better internally by developing skills and patterns of thinking and behavior that benefit you and the planet. Even if you are busy, even if you are afraid, even if you are confused, it is possible to reduce the worry and contribute to a more positive, loving, and kind environment. You do not have to feel it is overwhelming. Instead, begin to take small steps towards a happier you. The more people do this, the more light grows in the darkness.

Start by nurturing yourself by doing things that genuinely help you to feel that you are strong, kind, and wise. Perhaps you can teach others how to do this, or maybe you become a leader as you grow in the light, spreading it out through words, thoughts, actions, music, or caring. Your example of self-care helps others to care too. From this web of positivity comes new ways for many to live their lives and create a better earthly existence. Today is a good day to grow closer to the person you can imagine.

- Namaste -

Changing Course

You often seek to be reassured that all is well, that you are safe. Many times you look to see if there is something wrong with your life and the state of affairs around you. At these times, your confidence level is often low, and your balance is not stable. It is as though you are controlled by the constant passing of clouds and rainy weather.

These periods are of some benefit to you as they remind you of the need to make time to be of inner reflection, introspection, and contemplation of the self and the state of the world around you. You can be directed back to sitting in silence, walking in nature, and eating healthier during these times of disquiet. Instead of cursing or looking down on them, notice what is happening and give thanks for the reminder to change your course, direction, and focus.

Some come into your life on a close or distant basis, who come as teachers to help you learn the lessons you have chosen. These great teachers may appear as challenging, disrupting, and appearing to be negative forces. Instead, these beings seek to be the reminder of your need to change, grow, and focus on a healthier path. It is okay to give thanks to these, to show perhaps compassion, but then step away or set boundaries that protect and help you and others to change.

Today is a good day to find time to reflect and see things about yourself and the world from a wiser, more balanced perspective. Start or further your day with affirmations that increase your life force and energy. Be at peace.

- Namaste -

Healing Happens

Follow the heart's desire, and you will know much joy. Listen to your inner prompting to do the things you do. Set your intentions to become more aware, calm, loving, and at ease. Your affirmations of positivity are food for your growth. They nourish you and sustain you through all manner of challenging times. Your positive messages towards yourself help you to light up the darkness and illuminate your path.

There is much to be grateful for, including replacing negative thoughts, fears, and worries. Once you release a negative thought, you need to replace it with a positive. Crying tears of sadness allows you to cleanse your mind and body of toxic thoughts. Then filling up your mind and body with positive statements is like applying a soothing medication to a pain you have. Healing happens when you provide yourself with care and positive energy.

No one is without this need. This is part of being human, lessons to be learned. Judgment of yourself only furthers the issue. Letting the self process, emote, and then replace the negative with a positive is one way to heal. Today is a good day to set the intention to find positives to say to yourself all day long.

- Namaste -

No Separation

A whale in the ocean swims deeply into the dark of the water, yet it is not afraid. Instead, the whale feels peace and is at home as it is a part of its world of water. You also are a part of your world. Even though your worlds are very different, you can have understanding and compassion for this fellow creature, this fellow traveler.

All beings are made of similar stuff, the stuff that stars, planets, plants, rocks, and water are made of. There are universes within universes, so numerous that you are unaware that they exist. You are tiny, but you are also prominent. You are part of everything, and everything is part of you.

So much fear is baseless and unnecessary. You can focus on it or being part of the world inside and outside of you. Indeed, there is no separation at some level except what your fear creates. Being afraid is the forgetting of this connection to all. Nowhere is there separation from your Source. You are of Source, and Source expresses through you. You can be at peace as you sit or walk in silence. As you increase your ability to do this, you increase the knowledge of your connection and how it is expressed.

Today is a good day to sit or walk in consideration of the glory that is around you. Note to yourself how you are related to the people, animals, trees, rocks, etc. Look to see your connections, your likeness. Cultivate your peace.

- Namaste -

Take the Time

You are a soul among other souls. You are a person in a body that lives to be explored and studied. Your time in this body is finite, yet your soul and essence will never be destroyed. While you are here, you are invited to be on your chosen path. So every day, you walk into the unknown, the creation you and those around you decide to make.

Being a part of the world is a blessing as it enables you to explore, choose and carry out your intentions. You can be very dynamic with these options or become very quiet and peaceful with your options. Your life is built upon them as you go about the world. Are you spreading love and light? Is this your intention? You may need the time to decide what you want to do, contribute, or learn.

Today is a good day to look with fresh eyes at the world around you. What do you notice? What is your reaction? Is it pleasing to you? Do you take even a short time to reflect, relax, and empty your mind so that it becomes clearer what you want to accomplish? What do you want to be? Today is a good day and blessed day to evolve further you who is wise, kind, generous, calm, peaceful, et cetera.

- Namaste -

Find Your Treasure

To be happy, calm, and balanced, there is a path to follow that first of all values these things and then strives to be more skillful at their achievement. Self-discipline is valuable here as it helps in the development of the skills that you want and need.

Consider the athlete who must train to become better at their sport. They set their intention to become more skilled and succeed. Then they set regular time aside to run, swim, etc., so that they can practice for their success.

You, too, must set aside some time to practice relaxation, peaceful self-contemplation, and healing of your body, mind, emotions, and spirit. As you cultivate these treasures, you begin to grow the strength that comes from flexing the muscles of your inner peace.

Today is a good day to again put into play your plan to be centered, calm, and at peace. Sitting still and focusing on slow breathing is a good beginning for your practice. As you focus on your breathing and your mind and body calm, you become better able to be the person you desire to be. Starting with a short time and growing to longer times allows you to build up your skill. So if you desire, set aside time just for you, even if it is 5- to 10-minutes to start. Once or twice per day is a good beginning. May you feel the peace you seek.

- Namaste -

Self-Caring

There are many days when you may wonder if you are doing what you need to become the person you would like to be. Some days you may feel successful, and others not so much. It is as though you take a couple of steps forward and then a step or two backward, and keeping a perspective on your development is complex.

Because you are so engrossed in thoughts, emotions, and the physical world, you sometimes lose sight of your actual being, your true self. That is why it is important to balance yourself by stilling the outside world so that you can see what is going on, drawing together your mind, emotions, physical body, and spirit body. It is important to balance and respect all of these things. When you focus only on one or two of these aspects of yourself, you become out of balance. Then you can suffer from illness, mental lack of clarity, and emotional problems such as anxiety and depression. You may feel adrift and unconnected to any aspect of yourself.

It is beneficial to still all aspects, to calm them and be at peace. When you do so, you experience life much more positively and joyfully. Your health on all levels, whether mental, emotional, physical, or spiritual, improves. You become more skillful at expressing the true you, who is a fully integrated being. Then you can also help others comprehend and better develop their skills.

So, today is a good day to continue your practice of caring for and loving yourself. How you do this is up to you. Perhaps you pray, meditate, walk in nature, create or express a talent. There are many ways to balance yourself. May you find moments of realizing your joy along the way

. - Namaste -

Stoke the Fire

Yesterday is no more. It has been stored in the vault of time and memory. It is no longer the present, and yet its influence is still felt in the now. All beings live in many levels of time, memory, and energy. As you go about your day, you are influenced by the old, even as you change into the new.

Many are feeling this pull between the times, which is normal. Fears due to past influences are intense as you as a group try to decide and follow an ever-evolving path.

Now is an excellent time to reach out for peace and calm. Now is a good time to help others around you feel safe and their own peace and tranquility. No one is without the need for this so that they can see clearly and make decisions more wisely.

You can be that hope-generating person, but you must be sure to set your intention to be of light to all and then practice your sitting in silence. Teaching this to others is also of benefit as there are many who are open to it.

If you have fears, it is because you have forgotten love. If your thoughts are loving, you will banish fearful ones. All of you must remind yourselves of this as you confront your fears and those of others. Remember to nurture and develop the skills you need to be of lightness. Light dissolves the darkness of fear.

Today is a good day to set your intention to be of light, of loving kindness for you and others. Be the person who sets aside time to stoke the fire of your light. When it grows dim, remember to rekindle it into positive thoughts and affirmations.

- Namaste -

Your Image of Yourself

For those who choose, many opportunities exist to become more evolved and aware. Many options present themselves when you open yourself up to the flow of infinite possibilities, the field of energy you all dwell in, but few recognize.

You are, in a sense, limited only by how you choose to see the world and how you choose to interact with it. Your vision of possibilities has much to do with what happens or doesn't happen in your life.

Imagine that your thoughts set into motion a vibration felt throughout this field of energy, this field of possibilities, and what you send out returns, surrounds, enfolds, and is your reality. Learning to guide your thoughts and keep them as you want them is important. It may feel like herding cats, to begin with, but with practice, your thoughts and, therefore, your life will improve, and "miracles" will happen.

You are here in this body, this life, to become, to grow. You can become what you imagine, so it is a good idea to imagine yourself in positive, enhancing ways. The more you do this, the more it becomes real.

If you experience negative thoughts, recognize them as clouds that temporarily block your sun and energy channels. They are not the totality of your reality. Once you have dealt with them, replenish yourself with positive, calming thoughts. Let go of these to uplift yourself and others. Today is a good day to know that there is an infinite field of possibilities for you.

- Namaste -

Free Yourself

Being focused on spiritual growth is a goal that provides you with much that is satisfying and beneficial. Your desire to be a better person is a goal that leads you to new areas of thought, emotions, action, and awareness. When you genuinely desire this path, you may walk in ways that initially appear different or strange but become familiar and comforting over time.

You can decide in your life what you want to explore. The world around you may not see things exactly as you do, but this is okay. Being brave means that you choose to go the path that is yours and that suits you, not everyone else.

In today's world, many fears are around you. You are offered the opportunity to view these fears, and then you can choose to let them go as you would let go of your breath. As you experience fearful thoughts or emotions, you can develop the skill of first becoming aware of the experience. Then after observing it, you can let go of the fear and instead realize what it is and that you have the choice to free yourself from it. This process is a healthy one that helps you to stay calm and centered in times of fear and discord. Clouds come and go across the sky. Likewise, fearful thoughts come and go. Nothing stays the same. Observing is a necessary skill for peace in your life. Observe the clouds in your sky and be grateful for them, as they help you to know yourself. Their absence helps you to value the clear sky and your peace.

Today is a good day to set the intention to observe your thoughts when you can and grow in your ability to do so. Be kind and supportive of yourself as you would a child that learns to do the tasks it needs to mature. Today is a good day for compassion for yourself and others, as all are on the path to growth.

- Namaste -

You Choose

Abundance is yours, and each day, you must express your gratitude for all that comes to you each day. As you express your appreciation and concentrate on it, you open the channels and gates for your continued receiving of all that you need.

Everywhere about you is the field of infinite possibilities, and as you express your openness through gratitude, you attract the essence of what is good for you. On the other hand, complaining and focusing on anxiety attracts more of the same to you. Which do you prefer? More that gives you back joy or that which attracts sorrow? You get to choose what you get in many ways.

If you can take the time to sit and consciously give thanks for all that is yours, you create more happiness for yourself. Even giving thanks for things that appear negative has the effect of increasing your satisfaction. All that comes to you has a purpose. Even though your sight can be limited or your understanding not clear, you are nourished by all.

Today is a beautiful day to give thanks moment by moment as you experience life. Expression of acceptance and gratitude can increase your ease and joy in living. Be aware of each thing that you receive. Praying without ceasing means being grateful moment by moment. Setting your intention to do this will be rewarding.

- Namaste -

Start Your Adventure

How are you this morning, dear ones? Are you waking with the sun's rising to greet this new day? How is it with your eyes? Are they opening to see all around you, the physical glory?

You have awakened from slumber to again inhabit your body and live another day in your life. Are you ready for the new lessons you will work on? Is your heart open along with your eyes? Is your mind open along with your eyes and heart? Is your spirit awakened along with the rest of you?

Perhaps today is the start of new thoughts, new visions, and new experiences that you can embrace and accept within yourself. You are as though an adventurer setting off on a new, unknown path. How do you feel about this adventure? Can you feel your excitement, your curiosity about what scenery you will see, what new people you will come close to, and what new concepts you will learn? So many questions, but may your questions be answered in ways that astound you with the clarity of the day's messages, the day's purpose, and the day's blessings.

What will you take with you to set out on your daily adventure? What comes to mind? Do you settle on sturdy or light walking shoes? Do you take sustenance and health-providing provisions? Do you take an open and wondering mind that allows you the freedom to learn? Have you begun to see what it is you choose to do?

Today is a blessing. Today is yours to create. Today is now.

- Namaste -

Developing Healthy Habits

Many have barriers to overcome to grow and mature in life. These barriers are a normal part of your being and in no way mean that you are inferior or deficient, but rather that you have chosen to work on specific issues in this lifetime so that you may learn and grow. Judging oneself is not helpful in the end as this doesn't help you to grow and change. Barriers are not really barriers in that you can heal and change that which challenges you.

One beneficial strategy is to recognize the problem as an opportunity. Recognizing it is the first step, as you can't easily change what you don't see or own. This is often the hardest step, and many go their whole lives without seeing the challenges presented. Once this is done, it is important not to judge but to see the challenge as a way to help heal yourself. Then comes observing yourself and learning to be the observer rather than the reactor. One might see that they are acting according to an old pattern and then say, "I am reacting, there it is again, etc." Then, instead of feeling bad, you can change it to being glad to see the pattern. Once recognized, one can begin to remedy the challenge/problem. Sending loving and thankful thoughts to the problem and yourself is often a way to unblock the issue and allow healing.

The more you develop the habit of an insightful, loving response to yourself, the happier you will become. Another benefit is doing this towards others by seeing their patterns/challenges and not reacting, but changing your response to one of observation and loving care. Separation from some may be the result, but a part of your caring respect for yourself and the other person.

Today is a good day to notice what comes up for yourself and to observe rather than react. You are gaining ground each time you do this and catch yourself reacting.

- Namaste -

Be Still

Open yourself today to being the new you who comes to be. The universe and the Source so love you, and you are a part of all that is. Nowhere is there a place where you do not have the support of life and love. You begin to feel and understand how this can be when you sit in silence. Let yourself quiet enough that you can know that this is so.

You are never alone. You are always loved. You are a pinpoint of light. You are an entire universe of energy.

If you are very busy, take less time, but if you can, find time to regularly go to where things become clear, where fears and worries recede, and you KNOW the truth of your existence.

Follow this path that leads you to be awake, aware, and alive today. Set your intention to be still and know that you are the loved being that you are. It is your time to be present and to be a positive influence on the world around you. Be free, and be kind to yourself and others.

- Namaste -

Living in Abundance

Manifesting your abundance is a sign that your energy channels are unblocked and that you are functioning in a manner that does not impede your giving and receiving. When you are unblocked, you are better able to receive and give back to the order of things.

It is vital to keep yourself uncontested, as it were, to increase your flow of abundance. Abundance occurs at all levels-physical, mental, emotional, and spiritual. Your abundance is a direct sign or indication of how all of these systems are balanced. You can increase abundance as you increase your energy flow and connection with the Source. When you focus on yourself, you can set into motion greater abundance.

Setting aside time to focus on your inner balance is a good improvement strategy. Finding a way to sit in silence that works for you is beneficial. Even if you are in a busy life, prioritizing some time, however small, to go within and center yourself is helpful for your growth and abundance.

Giving thanks throughout your day is another tool to help you balance better. The use of physical practices such as yoga, Qigong, walking, etc. also is beneficial. So much can be done to increase your connection to Source and abundant living.

Today is a good day to work on your intention, be in balance, appreciate what comes to you, and recognize that you are in the flow of light.

- Namaste -

We Have Weather

Feeling good is a benefit of balancing your mind, emotions, body, and spirit. When all are functioning well, there is a more vital life force and joy. Being in the flow of prosperity is much more likely when all are balanced, and you are able to genuinely feel grateful. Being in better balance means better outcomes. It also means that when you experience being out of balance, you can grow into recognizing it and restore your balance more quickly.

The goal is not to be perfect but to be able to remedy the periods of time when you find it challenging to be in balance. If you were never out of balance, it would be more challenging to recognize being in harmony.

So, accepting yourself when you are shaky and have storm clouds that darken your sun is helpful. When you realize what is happening, you can say thank you for the lesson and the teachers and then return to use strategies that help you restore balance and peace.

Many become used to the storms and don't realize the reality of the calm. The more you achieve peace and joy, the more you can achieve it. Today is a blessed day for you. Today you can increase your joy, abundance, and prosperity of the mind, the physical, emotional, and spirit.

- Namaste -

The Force Is With You

Behind each of you is the helping hand of Spirit, of Source. For many, a sense of support is felt and acknowledged. The energy of love, that is, your support, is given to you so that you can radiate it and reflect it through yourself to the world around you.

No one is alone. Invariably, this force illuminates your body and the universe. No one is without this energy as it is the life force itself. It is the energy that is in your body and enlivens you.

When you are born, this energy enters your body and remains there until you die, and then it leaves your body. This energy is intelligent, and itself exists in some form forever. Changes happen to the being you call the self, but the essential spirit, the energy of Source, always exists.

Know that you have chosen to be in your body. Care for it, love it, and be grateful for it. Do not get lost in it and lose sight of your true self, which is much more than solely your body. Today is another day to learn, to grow in awareness and joy. Honor yourself by your intention to be in every way more alive and filled with understanding.

- Namaste -

Without Ceasing

Today is when you celebrate your existence and give thanks for everything in your life. You sense that there is more to this life than your physical pleasures. You are becoming more attuned to the possibilities around you, and you know that all that comes to you is an opportunity to rejoice and be glad.

You are on this journey and have the opportunity to be grateful for every breath, every experience, and every burst of energy. You are in joy when you look through the eyes of thankfulness and reaffirm all you are and will become.

You bless all you have been and give thanks for what has come. Let yourself feel the joy of gratefulness, not only on this day but on all days, all moments. Say thank you without ceasing. As you grow in your ability to be grateful, you grow in joy. As you grow in joy, you become more and more a radiator of love and kindness.

Today, pause to recollect all your memories, people, places, and times for which you can be thankful. Give them importance and respect. Give thanks for the present moment as it connects you to the past and future. May all be a blessing.

- Namaste -

The Gift of Dreams

Have you had dreams that intrigue you? Do you perhaps wake and wonder why you dreamt what you did? Have you had dreams that melt away while others stay with your thoughts and lend emotions to the beginning of your day?

You are not alone in this experience. All or most have dreams that they remember, at least from time to time, and in these dreams comes exciting information. Sometimes they reflect on previous experiences. Other times, dreams may show you future events. Some dreams comfort. Some disturb. Some just seem to be strange to you.

Your dreams reflect the topics with which you are often occupied. They may come to you as reflections of what you are dealing with in your growth. They may give you important information or be a jumble of random bits. All in all, you can thank your dreams for helping you to clear things in your subconscious. As they bubble to the surface of your mind, you can examine the thoughts and emotions produced.

Again, it helps to step back to observe once you have awakened. What is the theme here? What are my feelings? Do I feel directed to do something or to cease something? Am I feeling loved? Am I feeling confused? Am I feeling distressed or comforted? What if any sense or message comes from this? As dreams tend to fade rather quickly, it helps to record them if you can.

Today is a good day to give thanks for all of your dreams. They are a part of you. As you learn to love yourself more and more, you recognize the unique and valuable gift dreams are for you.

- Namaste -

Be the Gift

Probably, many will start today from the state of being relaxed and at ease. Many do this by practicing sitting in silence or moving into relaxing postures. It is helpful for the rest of the day if you can do this. The after-effects last for some time, and the more you cultivate the habit, the more you are likely to build up reservoirs of calm, peace, and balance.

There is the opportunity to grow into a new type of being than you have been in the past, a person who can relax more and more by intention. As it becomes more and more familiar to be content and at ease, you can extend the time spent in that space. You can flex your relaxation muscles with greater emotional ease.

This ability is essential, not only for you but also for those around you. Since all are connected, the ripples of your changes into this new way of being extend out and impact the whole of creation. You become the gift of positive influence for the world. Your being is, therefore, important no matter who or where you are. Your energy becomes part of the universal web of light and love.

Today is an excellent day to nurture your energy and grow your light. Setting the intention to calm down for a few moments is like putting money in the bank. In the end, all it can do is be the hope and light you seek

- Namaste -

You Are Eternal

Be aware in this moment that there come to you many ways to see the world and what happens in your life. Often there come times when you change the course of your thinking, and you look through new lenses to see what is there.

You can go about your day knowing that all is ever-changing, and even to the cellular level, you are in the wave of evolving, growing, and expanding. Your energy is from the Source, the universal reserve of light. It cannot be extinguished.

Today is a good day to set the intention to assist yourself in feeling your freedom. You can start this day's journey by affirming that you are eternal. Being in this mindset helps you to be able to observe rather than react. It allows you to step back into being more curious and content and notice what you are learning and what lessons you have chosen. Take yourself by the hand and lead yourself into the day.

- Namaste -

Gathering Information

You are designed to function properly in health. As you become more aware, you become healthier. As you do this, your sense of being connected to all increases. The information you can absorb, understand and use increases. You then move through life in a more satisfying and beneficial manner. Being in this state of grace or awareness is being aware of your true self beyond the many obstacles you encounter.

Finding and understanding the true self takes discipline and commitment to growth. Opening the mind, heart, and spirit to information that supports all things is necessary. The more you cultivate this knowledge, the more information will come to you. You recognize that information is in you, around you, and you are one with it.

Today is a good day to welcome more information and knowledge. Give thanks for everything that happens. Seek some time, however short, to sit in silence and listen. Your true self is always there.

Even though clouds hide the sun or daylight hides the stars, the sun and stars are still there. Even though daily life may do the same obscuring, your true self is still there.

- Namaste -

Time Realized

In many ways, you are being tested to become a stronger, more cohesive you. In these days of individual and group challenges, you are receiving and learning new information, not only about concerns and dilemmas but how to organize and utilize the time you have to be alive in your body.

It is not that you must be afraid of the limits of life, but that it can help you to realize that each moment, each day, each week, month, and year is precious time. If young ones were given this perception, of love, from the start of life, things would be much different.

You are not alive to squander your life, but many don't have the information they need to make sense of and use what is given.

It is good to gather your energy when you can, preferably early in each day, and attempt to set the tone so that it helps you focus. It also helps, throughout your day, to remind yourself of this tone that you have selected. Then as you move through the day, you can better take in and give out needed information.

At the end of your day, it is helpful to sit and gather yourself again, perhaps to review what has come to you. Training yourself to be aware this way is very beneficial to your growth and helps to satisfy the longing each of you has. Over time, you become less lost in the chaos and more comfortable with life.

- Namaste -

Never Done

Be on a quest! You are on a journey, seeking out that which is of benefit for your development. Perhaps this takes you outside to be involved with many others, or maybe you will be more cloistered and spend the time in relative isolation. No matter where you go or what you do, you are still on a journey to learn more about yourself and the world that you are living in.

The world is your classroom. Did you think you were done with your learning just because you were not formally in school? Hah! You are always in the school of learning. You never stop becoming more knowledgeable. Some try hard not to grow or change, but ultimately, this is impossible.

So, today is a good day to embrace the people, situations, thoughts, and feelings you experience with a sense of adventure and acceptance. Give thanks for all, because it is part of a glorious life offered to you. If things become difficult, rest and seek guidance, you need to move through it. You are never alone in life or in death. You cannot be as if you are a part of the universe, and it is a part of you. Today is a good day to see what is being taught with new eyes.

- Namaste -

Asked to Share

Fortune is an opportunity to share. When you are blessed with more than you can use, you are being asked to use your resources wisely to benefit not just yourself but all those in need. Your blessing is making you a change agent of distribution, and is meant to help allocate out to the world that which you do not need.

Many people attract these blessings but then get stuck in fear of losing what has been given. This fear blocks the ability to be balanced, and energy becomes out of alignment. Fear does not resolve the issue of flow but instead gets in the way, and deterioration ensues. This does not mean having abundance is terrible, but it needs to be a result of being in physical, mental, emotional, and spiritual balance.

As you become more balanced, you are asked to share, not just in the physical sense but in these other areas. If you are in balance, you cannot help but share your blessings with others.

Today is a good day to recognize the blessings that you have. Observing what these are and then giving thanks increases your abundance. Sending out the loving kindness bestowed upon you keeps its beneficial energy alive and well. Be of gratefulness for your countless blessings.

- Namaste -

Develop Your Practice

All about yourself is the rushing and busyness of life. In this daily running and busyness, you are easily snagged so that, like most others around you, you become lost in the web of being alive. As you enter the day, it is expected that forces call upon you to respond and to make choices that determine your course. Interwoven into this is your consciousness and that of all other beings. You and others create each day, each minute, each second, all that occurs. Often this is through processes that you are not aware of. Your choices and reactions become entangled so that reality is confused or disturbed.

We have spoken many times about the need to be still for a portion of time, preferably at the beginning of your day, to set your intention and balance yourself mentally, physically, emotionally, and spiritually. Without doing so, you run the risk of unconscious living. Your risk of illness, negative thoughts, emotions, and choices increase.

Prayer or sitting in silence (whatever you individually define it as) is the basis for growing into your wisdom. You are able to calm yourself and intuit more truly what is best for you, as well as those around you. As you progress in practice and skill, you are able to be more love-directed and happier.

Today is a good day to set aside your time for introspection, meditation, or prayer in whatever form suits you. Forgive yourself if you feel unable to do it, and set the intention to do it when able. Because of the speeding up of time and the challenges being created, it will benefit you greatly to be disciplined in this practice.

- Namaste -

Giving Thanks

Your independence is not what you think it to be. While you may feel that you can achieve this, it is really that you are interdependent. You are always connected to others, even if you are feeling alone.

Taking the being, you call yourself. You see that you could not have been born into this life without the union of your parents. You could not have survived without the care of others. Your interactions with others have sparked your growth and evolution.

Because others influence you, why not take the time each day to thank your ancestors, your parents, your siblings, extended relatives, friends, enemies, teachers, et cetera? Expressing your gratitude helps to ground you and open your heart to all.

Today is a good day to set the intention to be grateful and open your heart wide. Be of loving kindness to others and yourself.

- Namaste -

A New Year

As you end this year, you become a different person with a new path and view. You are starting out afresh to build more on your life. It is an opportunity to review the past year and decide what has worked well and what you might want to change.

How can you increase your joy or happiness if you are sad about how things have gone? If you have been dissatisfied, how can you increase your contentment? If you have been afraid, what can you do to improve your feelings of safety? You have more power than you often realize. You can become more of what you desire as you examine/observe and then set your intention.

Being aware of your need, affirming the positive, and sending out this message into the universal field of information, sets into motion your desire.

Be patient in this new year as you let go of your intention and then see the reality of it come to fruition. You do not need to control, and in fact cannot control, how this comes about. But your intentions and results go to what you ask for, where your mind is.

This is an excellent day to reflect on the past year and be grateful you had it to experience. Be joyful in the moments you experience during the new one, and be prepared to grow even more.

- Namaste -

Your Own Best Friend

Emotions are clues as to what works well for you and what doesn't work. You can tell from what you feel what thoughts are circulating in your mind. Perhaps you are feeling balanced, joyful, or confident. Or maybe you are feeling sad, anxious, or unhappy. Any of these are not really good or bad but simply indicators of how your mind's furnace is operating. Are you cultivating positive, self-affirming thoughts or thoughts that bring you down?

It is a skill to keep walking and thinking in an uplifting manner. When you are feeling either pleasant or unpleasant thoughts, you can become more aware that you are experiencing them.

Then perhaps you can see yourself as you would a friend. How could you assist this friend in feeling and thinking in a healthy and balanced way? Balancing doesn't mean that you always feel the same but that you get more skillful at not deviating to extremes.

Today is a good day to be supportive of yourself. Relate to yourself as you would to someone you are encouraging. Be kind, be supportive, and be your own best friend.

- Namaste -

In the Flow

Placing yourself in the flow of good or abundance is another skill that can be developed.

As you begin to see the correlation between thoughts, emotions, and your abundance, your reality, you start to see that what you are manufacturing becomes the reality you receive.

If you can cultivate a more positive and loving reality, you will receive much more positive results. Even if adverse events occur, you will be able to handle them and, over time, will prosper greatly. This happens at all levels of your life.

Today is a good day to set your intention to see the day in a more balanced way. Choose thoughts that please you. If you notice a negative pattern, replace it with a higher perspective. Don't judge yourself, just focus on raising your skill level.

- Namaste -

Laugh

Laughter can explode from you like an eruption of joy. Laughing is a skill that can be developed and is useful in maintaining your health and happiness. While some have a more natural ability to laugh and find life enjoyable, everyone can learn to be better at laughing.

Taking time to see the world as a funny place helps you to be relaxed and content. Cultivating laughter assists you physically, mentally, emotionally, and spiritually in developing into a person who can be free of many fears and concerns. If something comes along that normally might be of concern, you can choose to be in fear or laugh at this thing instead. Cultivating laughter takes the sting away from many events and allows you to see the drama for what it is, drama and not such a powerful thing.

Today is a good day to nurture yourself by getting yourself to laugh at what comes along. You can do this while getting ready for the day, driving in your car, or taking a shower. Starting to practice in private may be a first step in lightening the burdens you don't want to carry. Laugh and be full of joy.

- Namaste -

Calm and Clear

Your innermost calm depends significantly on your ability to become quiet in your thought processing. When you become calmer in your body, your thoughts become calmer too.

By accessing calmer energy for either your mind or body, you are more successful in being peaceful. As you become this calm energy, your ability to see more clearly is accentuated. Your mental process is helped to be clearer, and your body becomes healthier.

Constant rushing and being overly busy makes for a stressed mind and body. Too much for too long is not suitable for you. Setting up a culture of calmness is better for your longevity. All areas benefit and become better at not being negatively influenced.

Today is a good day to cultivate calmness, even for a short time. Finding some time in your day to settle into it is a good plan for your health. Be good to yourself.

- Namaste -

Open to Guidance

Today is a good day to be grateful for all that is given to you. If you can cultivate this particular attitude, you are blessed beyond all that is. Being grateful is the skill that helps you to be content and peaceful. When you are able to be thankful, you attract more to you to be grateful for. The energy of gratitude is a higher one and helps you and those around you to live in a healthier vibration.

Today is also an excellent day to put your trust in the light and love of the universe. Asking for guidance and allowing yourself to be led is another skill that can permeate your day and your path.

As you walk your day, ask for the right things to do or say. This inner wisdom is the light that leads you. As you grow in trusting this guidance, you become more connected to the Source. You are guided by it and less and less by ego or fear.

Today is a good day to set the intentions to be grateful and open to guidance. It will make your path a more joyous one. -

Namaste -

Choose a Different Path

Progress is made whenever you can seize the moment and change a negative thought for a more positive one. Anyone is capable of this skill, which greatly affects how you feel.
When there are times of dispute or times of illness, you can turn to make your thoughts more aligned with joy, love, and kindness. Perhaps this doesn't sound reasonable, but having more happiness and satisfaction is possible.

You are already halfway to your goal if you become aware of negative thought patterns. It is beneficial to help yourself welcome thoughts that can be of a different vibration.

Many are the ways to do this. You are able to choose which ones work for you. Perhaps you can go out in nature or sing songs that change your vibration. Perhaps there is a physical routine that allows you to focus on the moment and change your breathing to a slower rate. You may desire to engage in a creative act that will enable you to channel the energy of love and joy into the making of something. So many options are there for you to turn your thoughts into ones that decrease your pain and suffering.

Today is a good day to put energy towards this end. Allow yourself to become aware of it and choose a different path or train of thought.

- Namaste -

Request Assistance

You are in this world to learn, grow, and become more aware of who you truly are.It is important to ask for assistance as you walk your path. When you request assistance from the Source, you open yourself to more possibilities. As you go about your day, you become able to access and become more aware of all that goes on around and within you. This intention is important to your development.

Today is a good day to begin with, this intention. Take a few moments to give thanks, be grateful and ask for the Source of light and love to be there to guide you and support you throughout your day. Then go into your day with the assurance that you are strong yet flexible.

- Namaste -

Seek the Truth

You are on a journey that will take you through many interesting landscapes. Your time in your life is spent wandering the hills and valleys of your consciousness.

At times you feel exhilarated and, at times, weary, but always you are going out to be alive and to be enlightened. To be enlightened is to bravely approach your life as it is and seek the truth about yourself and others.

You are going about your life not to be perfect but to understand and accept who you are. Because you are connected to all, you also grow in your understanding and acceptance of others. It is all tied together.

Today is a good day to become more aware of yourself and your path. You can set your intention to be in the space to see with open eyes and accept yourself in all aspects. You become much more content, happy, and kind to yourself and others when you can do so. Today is a good day to love yourself.

- Namaste -

You Are Perfect

When you tackle the chore of the work of becoming more aware, you need not stress or become overwhelmed. Coming to fruition with your development takes time and doesn't happen overnight.

Your life is spent building the foundation of your beliefs and your skills. You become wiser and more skillful as you walk your path. You cannot start and expect to be perfect. Instead, you become aware of your need to learn and grow, and then you accept that you are perfection even as you evolve.

You are the manifestation of perfect Source energy. As such, you cannot be anything but perfect. You are the energy that is the foundation for all that is. Your love for yourself and all else grows as you become more aware of this connection.

Today is a good beginning for the awareness that you are in the process of building your reality. Build your reality by repeating throughout your day, "I am part of all that is."

- Namaste

Effortless Flow

Precision is the key to your going forward in this time. It is precision that is the goal of developing your energy system.

As you guarantee that you take the time to relax, to go within to contemplate your true self, you set the mold for your growth. Setting the mold does much to formulate the precision of your structure. Your structure is the basis for your strength and your abilities.

As you become more adapted to this relaxation, this inner peace, you become more fluid in your ability to be at one with all that is. You can then flow with the sea of creation. Dams may appear but are more easily unblocked. Your mental, physical, emotional, and spiritual health, and well-being increase.

This is where true power originates from, not in constriction and holding tight, but in effortless flow and flexibility of energy from the Source.

Today it would be to your benefit to set your intention to achieve as much calm and connection to your inner self as possible. It is your money in the bank, as it were. Stop, affirm and go within in the ways that work for you. You are precisely where you need to be and doing what you need to do.

- Namaste

Light Energy

You live much of your time unaware of your true self. You become very concerned about fears and depend upon unstable ideas for living your life. This is not a bad situation, but it only indicates your developmental level.

You would not expect a child starting school to be able to accomplish the same tasks as one who is graduating. So, accepting where you are is beneficial. You become more evolved, and as you progress, you become more accepting of yourself and others.

If you choose to sit or walk in silence, you can better recognize your inner wisdom and connect with the knowledge of more profound truths. As you connect more and more with the truth about yourself and the universe, you become more illuminated by the universal energy field. Becoming more aware of this is part of your purpose for being. As you become more mindful of this connectedness to creative energy, you can do things that would have previously seemed impossible

Today is an excellent day to affirm that you are a being of light and that this light energy gives you life. Voicing gratitude opens you to expressing your power. Look for proof of your energetic expression. Observe and give thanks. This opens you to even greater knowledge.

- Namaste -

A Guarantee of Safety

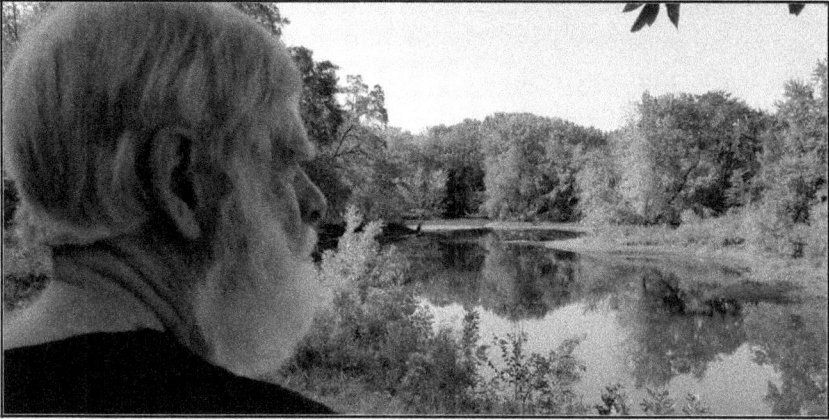

Safety is not what you may think it is. Safety is not the absence of challenging events. Safety is not protection from experiencing pain or lack. Instead, safety is a concept that goes beyond this. You will continue to have challenges in this physical world. It is not a sign of something being wrong with you. Instead, challenges may assist you in growing and becoming a stronger, more developed person.

You may want to see safety differently. A desire for security often comes from a fear of death, a fear of the ending of all you are and know. But in truth, you can never end. You are an eternal being. Your soul will continue after your body and this life cease. Therefore, you, the inner truth, the real you, doesn't have to be afraid. Your safety is guaranteed. The energy you cultivate and grow is never in danger of ceasing to exist.

Today is a good day to begin to see yourself in a new and liberating way. Be at peace. You can affirm to yourself that you are always safe.

- Namaste -

The Present Moment

You are healed every time you connect to the present moment. Your being becomes open then to all the energy that is available to you. You are centered in yourself and are able to receive the vital energy that comes from Source. And you become aware of this. When you become aware of this, you can't help but feel ecstatic with loving feelings and clearer thoughts are yours.

Being present is another skill that can be learned and practiced. Paying attention to your breath helps you to focus on the present. It helps you to relax and become aware of the moment instead of all a random thoughts that come to you.

Today is a good day to practice focusing on slow deep breaths whenever you can. You can do this while driving, while meeting with others, while sitting. The opportunities to breathe this way are endless. Perhaps you choose to count while breathing in-and-out or perhaps you pay attention to the up-and-down movement of your belly and chest. There are many ways to practice. This breath focus is beneficial to you on all levels. Have fun with it.

- Namaste -

Possibility

Thrilling is the concept of a new day. Grateful are you for the birds beginning their singing outside. Over and around you is the awareness of all that becomes possible with the sun rising.

You may feel gratitude for being in your body again. It is a gift to be awakened to live another day. You have the opportunity to become aware of more. You have the chance to think, feel and practice your skills in consciousness.

Today is a good day to learn and grow. Like the new spring growth, seeds planted within you are sprouting and developing roots.

You are on your way to becoming a new awareness, a new way to live your life. Today is a good day to give thanks for anything that comes to you.

- Namaste -

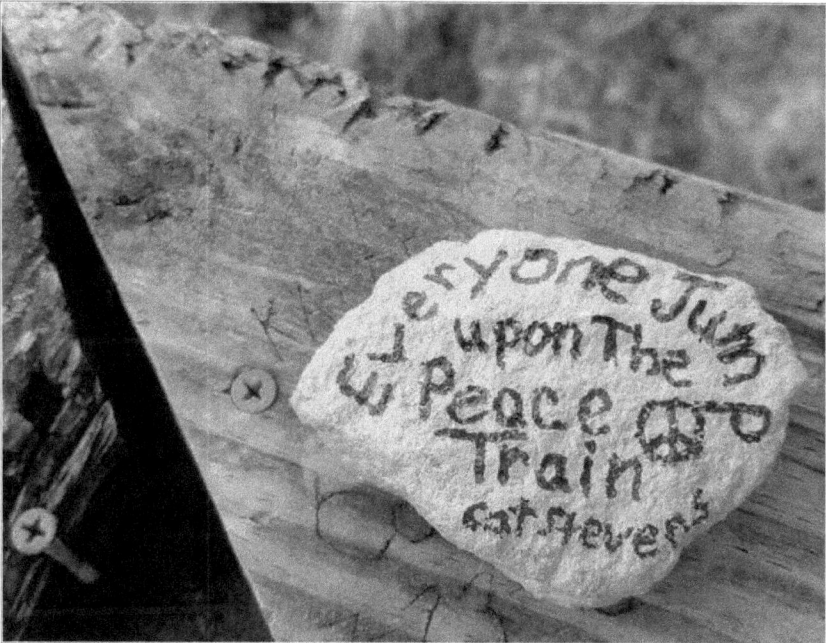

Understanding Yourself

Your past is not the cause of your future. You are not in alignment with the past as the source of what you are. Every moment is more the key to focus on, as it is the only time that truly is.

The past does not control you, but you can focus on what is occurring now. You are unlimited in your choices in dealing with what happens to you in the now. Because of this ability to choose in the now, you do not have to worry about the past. You do not have to judge yourself for anything. You are capable of and actually cannot help but evolve into the new you in each moment.

Because you may not recognize this change, you may not realize how much you have grown in your development, but make no mistake, you are growing and learning and becoming closer to the true self, the real you.

Seeing this development of yourself is an excellent gift as it allows you to give love to yourself. Understanding yourself is the basis for happiness. It also allows you to accept, understand, and care for others you recognize as growing, developing beings.

Today is a good day to take time to focus on the now moment as often as you can. Realize that you will go in and out of being able to do so, which is okay.

- Namaste -

Accept the Process

Your journey through life is meant to be one of growth and learning. Naturally, it follows that there must be areas of yourself that are not perfected and need growth and maturation.

Accepting this fact about yourself is valuable in helping you to grow. It is not necessary to be perfect or beyond the need to learn. You never can get to that which is static and beyond the process of growing and changing.

It is helpful to give yourself the freedom, the credit for being who you are at any moment. You are perfect in your imperfection. Other people around you are also growing and adapting.

If you can begin to see this reality and accept yourself and others as fluid beings, you will be better able to further your growth and those you come into contact with. This gives you a sense of acceptance of yourself and others. Your happiness increases with self-awareness.

Today is an excellent day to become aware that your challenges are opportunities for you to learn and grow. Give thanks for what and who comes your way.

- Namaste -

A Daily Miracle

When you rise in the morning, you return to the consciousness of being alive and in your body again. This is a great gift that may appear to be mundane, but it is indeed a miracle each time it happens. To be alive on another day is the gift you are given to further yourself and learn even more than the previous day. It may appear to be just another day, but it is unlike any that has come before, its possibilities are endless. Because you have this opportunity, you must be aware of your choice as soon as possible.

You can set the tone for your day before rising from bed. As you become aware, you can begin to greet the day by expressing gratitude for being alive and able to experience it. You can tell yourself what you are grateful for and thus become a positive force. Then as you go about your day, remind yourself of all there is to be grateful for. As you move throughout the day, you will find much to notice and give thanks for.

Today is a good day to rise in the knowledge that you are blessed. You are going forward in learning the skills of life.

You can change your energy to have a higher vibration when you sit in silence. You can start the day in a better state of being and therefore begin the day better. Doing so has a lasting effect on all that you do throughout the rest of your day.

Because you choose to start the day this way, you are taking better care of yourself. If you make this a priority, you set the tone for self-care that allows you to do more and be more. If you make sitting in silence at the start of your day the pattern, you will see, over time, positive results.

So, set aside time at the beginning of your day to sit in silence today. If you cannot start today, start tomorrow. Let this simple act transform your energy.

- Namaste -

Set a Pattern

You are a mystery, and in this time you seek to understand yourself in more depth. You are an ever-growing and evolving being. You are not static. So every day there are new things to notice about yourself. It is not known, therefore with absolute certainty, what you will do or how you will act with others. You have tendencies. Still, you are also a fluid form of energy that seeks its way toward greater skills and knowledge.

Today is a good day to celebrate the new person you woke up to become. Putting lack of skills and mistakes from previous days behind you sets you free to move ahead into newly charted water. You can set intentions for the day and observe how things progress. Give thanks for being aware and awake.

- Namaste -

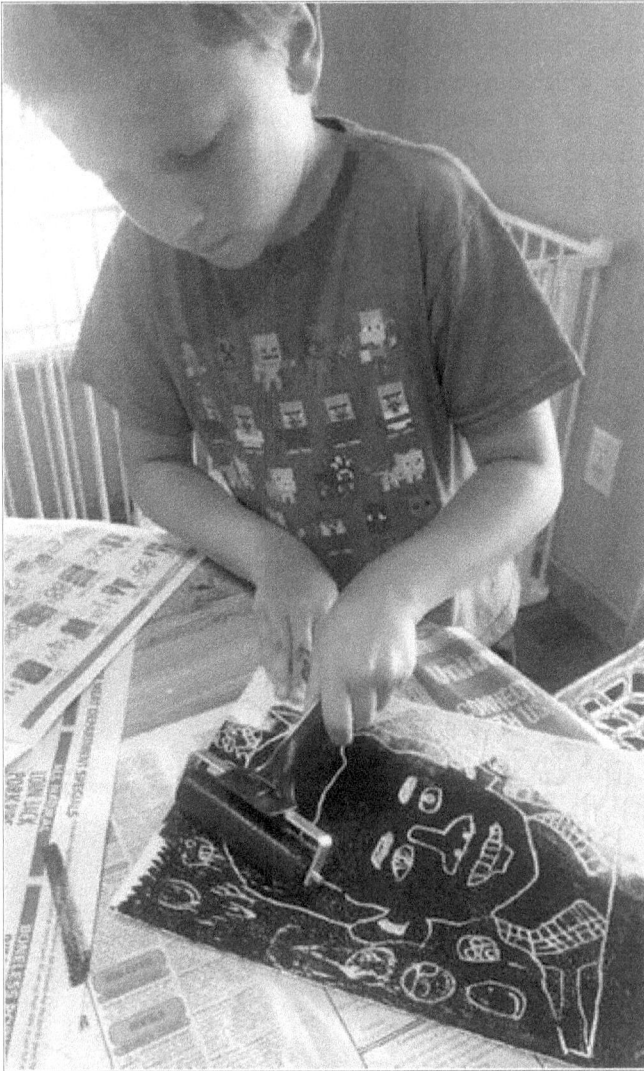

Energy Management

Your energy is what keeps life going in your body. You are fueled by this life energy that influences your body's systems.

You can feel the ebb and flow of this energy. At times you may feel full and, at times, feel almost empty. When you are full of the life force, you can think, feel, move and know all manner of things. Low life energy makes it challenging to think, feel, do, and learn.

It is important to keep your energy from becoming too high or too low. Neither extremes benefit you. Maintaining a more even energy level is a good goal or intention. Awareness is the beginning of the process of energy maintenance. Notice how and when you are feeling energetic. No judgment needs to be used. Just notice and practice acceptance of where you are at any time. You are perfect in all aspects

- Namaste -

What You Search For

The irony of your day is that while you live for it, you also try to escape from much of it. You come to the dawn, and you sigh because you must rise from your bed, yet if you were to stay there for too long, you would be longing to get up.

Could it be said that being satisfied or content is what you desire? Could it be that you desire to be calm and to know peace, yet you run from thing to thing?

Your searching is not for worldly success but rather the state of being where you are in touch with, recognize, and live with the knowledge of your true self. When you catch glimpses of this, you know it to be the path you seek, that all seek.

Today is a good day to focus on finding this calm, this contentment, this peace. How you do this can take many forms, but if you know of ways you have used in the past, you have only to remember them and bring yourself back to the tried and true. If you find yourself without this focus, be kind to yourself and take a few moments to nurture it again. You are blessed to be aware of your true self.

- Namaste -

Why Me?

You are blessed with drops of life-affirming water when the rain comes down. Be sure to give thanks for this blessed weather. Drought helps you to realize the value of each raindrop that comes your way.

Other challenges also come to help you learn about differences in perspective. Perhaps they help you to change in significant ways. At the time, these challenges may appear to be negative, and you may not be able to see their benefit. Later, with distance from the process, you begin to see where there may be value in it for you.

Today is a good day to be saying thank you, thank you, thank you for anything that comes to your mind. Perhaps your intention is to actively look for things you can see as blessings. The more you train yourself to do this, the more blessings come your way.

- Namaste -

Love Energy

Radiating love is a task for all of you. It is a part of your destiny on Earth. You are all imbued with this ability to center and balance yourself and your energy so that you can share your energy with others. This is not a superhuman ability but is one all can accomplish.

You can center yourself and reach a balanced energy state. This energy is the love that makes up the universe and all in it. You don't manufacture it; instead, you become aware of it and how to stay in touch with it more and more.

Today is an excellent day to calm yourself in ways that work for you. In your calmness, ask for the energy of love to be a part of your body, home, community, earth, solar system, galaxies, and the universe. Set your intention to share this loving energy with yourself and everyone you meet today. Go out in love and peace.

- Namaste -

Walk the Path

Often you harbor feelings that are not loving towards yourself and others. When this happens, your energy depletes, contributing to your lack of physical, mental, emotional, and spiritual health. Your ability to be calm, relaxed, and loving is not only decreased, but you can become stuck in a rut of negativity.

There are ways to cultivate a more positive and loving life. This life is more successful than one that depletes you and the world around you. If you set your intention to walk this more positive path, new opportunities to learn will come to you.

Today is a good day to seek to balance your energy. Sitting in silence will help, over time, to reset or retrain your brain. It will assist you in evolving into a life with less negativity. Many activities can help to balance your energy and uplift your life. Allow yourself these glimpses of what can be.

- Namaste -

Not a Contest

You are forgiven of all your mistakes and can become more at ease with yourself and the world around you. All of us are here to learn and grow. No one is perfect. As none are perfect, which is to say, without the need to grow and learn, you do not have to judge yourself or others so harshly. Seeing this as truth helps you to look at the world in a more relaxed and accepting manner. Often your mind is so focused on what is wrong that you cannot see what is going well. Your mind has these constant clouds of thoughts that move across your vision. If too thick, they block the light that sustains your life.

Today is a good day to observe what you see with the intention of acceptance and tolerance as often as possible. Again it is not a contest, and you are not competing with anyone. Instead, you are allowing yourself to consciously learn and grow. It is the purpose of your life.

- Namaste -

A Vital Part

You can't be in this world without it affecting you and you affecting it. Your being here on this planet, in this time, is the gift of life. In carrying on in this time, you have agreed to be a vital piece of creation. Your doubts, fears, and flaws do not prevent you from being a blessing and receiving many blessings. It is not that you become perfect but that you are always perfectly evolving. No one achieves perfection and stops growing. Accepting yourself is the way.

Looking back through the photographs of your years, you can see more clearly how you have changed, not just physically but also intellectually, emotionally, and spiritually. Be prepared to laugh and gasp at the changes brought by your growth.

Today is a good day to be at peace with yourself and all the choices and growth that have led to this moment, the next, and the next.

- Namaste -

Make the Link

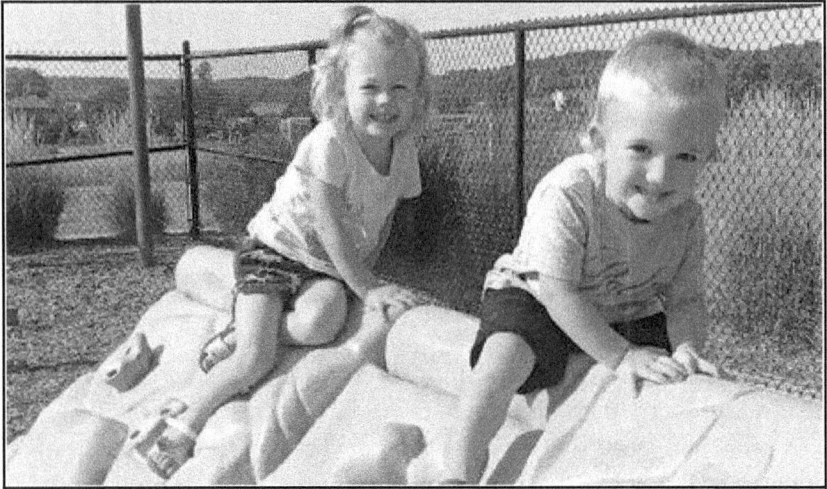

In this time, you are called upon to become more than you have been before. You are needed to be a force for the best energy you can present to yourself and others in the world. Everywhere is the opportunity to help better the lives of you all.

You need not diminish the importance of each of you. All are required to be of connection and help to each other. You are like a piece of paper in an endless chain that the children make. You are essential in keeping it all together. Instead of asking for your viewpoint to be the most important one, ask how you can help in any situation to make the links between you more robust and vital. By doing so, you help to keep the peace and allow all to evolve.

Today is a good day to practice saying words of hope, happiness, joy, and contentment. Be the link in the chain that does not give way but helps the world to stay together.

- Namaste -

Be the Peace

You see in these days that many are unhappy. They are talking harshly to each other about all kinds of things. Their fear of each other is being raised, so many do not accept others. When you feel caught up in this, you can extricate yourself and become peaceful, calm, and happy again. Like a bad habit, you can become drawn into it and even stuck in this type of fear. It may seem real. Your ability to handle and even help the situation is furthered when you change your mental and emotional states. Becoming a part of the angry mob does not help and decreases your effectiveness.

Today is a good day to focus on yourself. You know many ways to balance yourself and achieve a relaxed state. Remove yourself from situations that may stir up fears and instead cultivate times throughout your day that nourish you. Let go of negative influences that perpetuate fear and seek out what helps you to be calm. It is then that you can discern the truth.

- Namaste -

The Cycles of life

Your evolution is constant. Your growth can never be stopped. In each moment, you become someone different than who you were the moment before.

When you look at the rings of a tree, you can easily observe its growth. When you observe the layers in a cliff wall, you can see its development over time. In both, you can see times of significant change and less dramatic times. Your own growth is like this too.

Sometimes you are very thick, very much in a growth spurt. Sometimes, you feel like you are standing still and growing very little. Both are a part of your changing and evolving. Judgment is not needed, for both are normal.

Your change is constant, even if it feels as if you are standing still. It helps to give yourself credit for each breath, thought, emotion, and awareness that comes to you.

Today is a good day to recognize and praise yourself for your growth, whether a blazing fireball of progress or a lazy river of being. You are perfect in whatever cycle you are in.

- Namaste -

Your Bag of Tricks

Are you feeling overwhelmed by all the concerns in the world, your own life, and the life outside of you? Does your brain ruminate on issues that are causing you to fear? Does it feel like you are constantly anxious or, possibly, hyper, doing so many things? If so, it is beneficial to set your intention to change your thinking to become more at peace, to express joy rather than fear. Even becoming aware of this cycle of anxiety or fear is a good step toward changing it. As you become aware of it, be sure not to judge yourself for it, as it does not help but can hinder you.

Today is a good day to set your intention to relax, to eliminate or reduce fears and concerns. Many ways exist to do this, and as you age, your bag of tricks increases your physical, mental, emotional, and spiritual health. Perhaps you can listen to music and sing along. Or go for a walk. Do a physical practice such as yoga or Qigong. Maybe you can meditate or engage in something creative. Whatever you choose, allow it to change you and uplift you. Know that these things chase away dark clouds so you can feel the sun on your face again.

- Namaste -

Caring For Your Energy

There is a more wonderful existence than you have been aware of for you. In this time, you are called upon to learn a better, balanced way of living, one that fulfills you more and is beneficial to all around you. You are not just a body with a brain, a heart, a stomach, et cetera. You are a being in the universe. Both it and you are of one reality. You are not just a physical form but a being filled with the energy that runs and creates the universe you dwell in.

Because you are more than the physical, it is your job to be as receptive to receiving the energy as possible. This takes maintenance of and care-taking of your life force, your energy. To do this, you must allow opposing forces and energy to transmute into positive energy. How to do this? Each person is unique, but there are many ways to reach your highest energy flow. Yoga, meditation, nature, music, and so on are all good for balancing and recreating or maintaining your positive energy.

Today is a good day, as are all days, for nurturing yourself in healthy ways and practices that build your energy resources. As you do this daily, you will see the benefits. This will transform you.

- Namaste -

Increase the Peace

You are at this time being tested as to your courage and skillfulness. It is a time of turmoil all around you. It is your response to this that is the test. Are you able to not become caught up in chaos? Are you able to contribute to peace instead? Are you able to forgive yourself when you are not able to do this?

All are trying to make sense of the world and life. Many have no skills or support for learning to be of peace. Instead, many react and become part of the turmoil. They may withdraw and be of low energy. It is possible to increase your quota of peace, to share this peace with others.

Today is a good day to set your intention to find as much peace as possible. As you become more peaceful, you can influence the stability around you. Others can be attracted to this energy of peace you have to share. Make finding moments of peace an essential part of your day.

- Namaste -

A Channel of Love and Light

You are meant to be a beacon of light in a dark room. The eternal nature of your soul allows you to shine throughout all time on whatever stage you find yourself on. Seeing this role for yourself helps you to present positive, life-affirming energy to others who interact with you. You can go into many scenes to be a calming yet energizing influence.

You may be called to go into many places and even wonder why you are there. But do not worry. Instead, know your role is to channel love and light into the dark corners of existence.

Today is a good day to practice this role on the stage of your intention to be of help to others. Everywhere you go abides the opportunity to imagine light and love filling the space and driving away shadows. You are more important than you think.

- Namaste -

The Music of Sound

The sound of the chimes ripples out into the day further than your ears can detect. The energy spreads out beyond you and what your ears can hear.

Think then about how the sounds you make become energy that flows out from you into what you call the void. All around you is this area that carries the energy of sounds. Some hear this and make it into music that people can sing or play.

Sound energy is at a vibrational level and is associated with colors. Colors and sound dance together.

Today is a good day to listen to the sounds and the music in the world around you. Hear it in the traffic. Hear it in the rain and wind. Hear it in the song of birds and crashing waves. Wherever you are, there is this music of sound. Sitting in silence, you can hear it as your heartbeat, breathing in and out. Enjoy the variety and beauty that surrounds you.

- Namaste -

Make the Way Clear

Searching for peace is what many do these days. Peace is where negative energy is gone, and you can see more clearly what you need to see. When you reach this peaceful state, you can become more of what you desire to be. Your path is made more apparent, and you can walk it with grace and nobility of being.

Here in this time on Earth, there is the need to become a bearer of peace. When enough of you are present, you help to dispel the lower energies that drive negative actions.

When you sit in silence, asking for and sending out the energy of light and love is helpful. See it ripple through the Earth and beyond. Feel it restoring harmony to the swirling of all creation.

Today is a good day to increase your true wealth, the treasure of peace. As you nurture peace within you, be assured that you do the work that benefits not only you but all else around and beyond you.

- Namaste -

Share It With the World

Your voice can fill the world with much love, with much light. When you balance yourself and are filled with the energy of light and love, you can shine it and share it with the rest of the world. Some write beautiful songs, and others sing them. This helps many to be uplifted. You can do the same by simply saying words of hope and kindness to yourself and others. Everyone can inspire the world with their loving light.

Today is an excellent day to gather your love, light, and profound energy and give it to the world. See yourself going out and spreading it wherever you go.

Imagine it going before you and filling the places you are planning to travel to, then when you reach the places, give thanks. See yourself touching others, however briefly, with this bountiful and inspiring energy.

- Namaste -

A Change in Tactics

Often there comes to you a challenge that, by its nature, is perplexing, and you wonder how to handle it. What to do? This situation or this type of situation is prevalent for all people. It is unclear what you should do, and you become anxious about it. In times such as this, it is best to use the skills you have at your disposal.

Often people forget that they already have learned skills that can help them in the present moment. Instead, they focus on what is not going well. It is beneficial to stop the rumination on lack and instead train yourself to become more aware of your strengths to come to a more peaceful resolution of the challenge.

Today is a good day to cultivate this change of tactics for resolving issues you face. You can recognize that you are thinking thoughts that do not help you. You can ask for help to guide you to a better decision or result. You can seek out a calmness of mind and emotions so that you make the best choice. Practice giving yourself credit for being the capable person you are.

- Namaste -

A New Frontier

Treasures there are for you at this time. They are hidden away inside the vastness of your interior being. The uncharted, unexplored inner you contain much yet to be discovered by you. You are the explorer of yourself. You are on a journey to find what exists in the interior of the being called You. Often you are so absorbed in daily tasks of making a living that you become distant from you that it is more than a job, more than a role, more than a function, more than a task to complete.

When you sit in meditation or prayer, you begin this exploration, mapping the country that is you. No one is immune from the tug between exploring the outer and the inner world.

Today is a good day to create the journey and acknowledge that there is a new frontier for you to explore and treasure. You are being called upon to be your own traveling companion.

- Namaste -

Recognizing Connections

All of your experience in the world is going on in each moment. Even though you feel separate, you are always connected with and in touch with each other's energy. In a sense, you are one significant entity, one prominent being. You have unique facets that shine like the facets of a diamond, but you are still a part of the gem.

When you notice that you are experiencing a realization of a connection, give thanks, for it is a true gift in this place of veiled reference. When you see how connected you are, you develop the skill of being kind and compassionate. With this comes the ability to deepen your love of yourself and others. Your insight into connection shows your increase in knowledge and skill.

Today is a good day to practice this recognition of connection. Look around you, outside of yourself, and see who is there. Who waves, who smiles, who asks for help? What are your links to nature today? How are you inspired to interact? Open your heart and mind.

- Namaste -

Use Your GPS

In seeking out your path for life, you are often at odds with the atmosphere surrounding you. You wonder why you are where you are or why things occur. You often sense there is a way forward different from what you have been taught, but it is beyond your vision. You become involved with worldly tasks and issues and forget what you came here for.

We suggest you take the time to orient yourself the way you would on a journey where you need your GPS to get you to your destination. Sitting or walking peacefully helps to set your app for walking your path.

As you become more skilled in accessing this information, you will be rewarded with a more joyful journey.

Today is a good day to be aware of the opportunity to balance yourself so that you can be free to walk your path with better results and in a more peaceful mood. Sit with your internal GPS and let it guide you along your way.

- Namaste -

Exploring Unknown Territory

You are still exploring the unknown territory that is you. Your inner map is not complete. You continue to explore each day and create for yourself the adventure of walking your path, of creating this life you are living. When you sit in meditation or prayer, you go into the limitless landscape inside you. This landscape is a very fruitful one to explore and cultivate.

While you sit, the energy of light and love fills you like the sun rising and illuminates your being and your journey. This greatly assists you in walking your walk, in talking your talk.

Perfection is not the goal of your journey, as there is no such thing. Instead, you become more skillful, more knowledgeable. What you discover along the way becomes a part of you to take along with you and nourish you. Today is a good day to set aside time, however long, to explore and delight in your inner journey. Seek your inner sun.

- Namaste -

Make New Skills But Keep the Old

Sometimes you may feel discouraged about your health, the state of the world, or your relationships. Sometimes, joy is at low tide. At these times, your self-care practice is even more useful. It is not harmful to feel down or at low tide, but it is a communication that you are being challenged to use skills you have long forgotten or laid aside. Often those skills are waiting in the wings for you to acknowledge and use again.

Life often presents pop quizzes where you are asked to remember and use your skills. There are also times that call out to you to learn new ways to help yourself grow and balance. This can be exciting, especially if you recognize what is happening. Today is a good day to honor wherever you are and whatever you are feeling. Look to the message in the communication. Seek out the skills you already know and find new ones you need.

- Namaste -

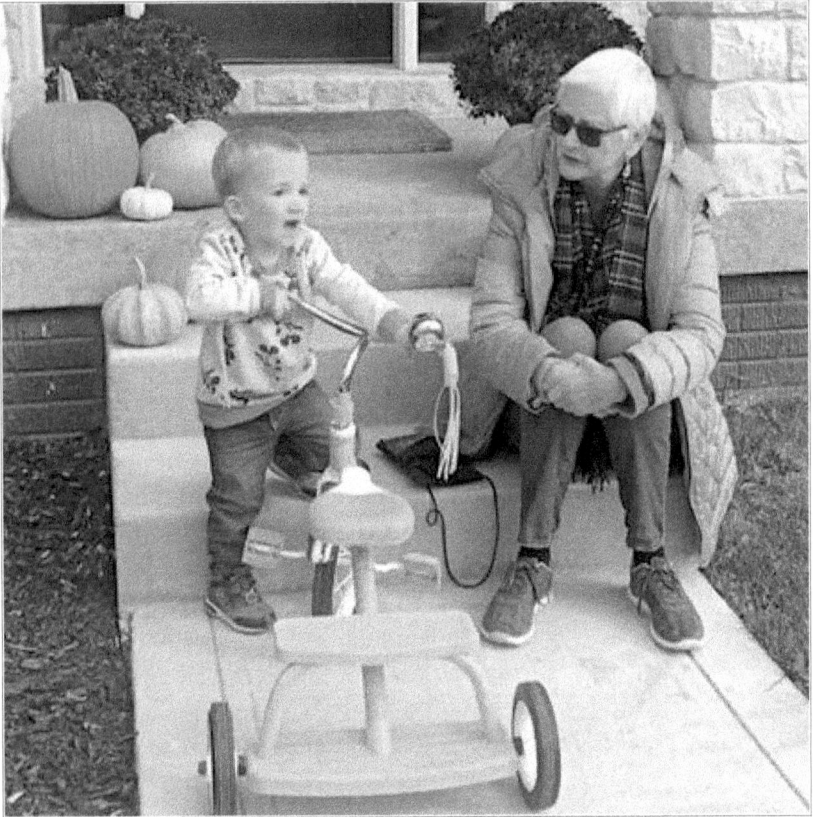

Commit to Knowing Yourself

False living refers to the unconscious state of being that many dwell in. This state of being does not define you but can control your development so that you develop more slowly than necessary. When you commit to knowing yourself in the sense of being free of fears, your cells undergo tremendous change. Your mind becomes clear, and your emotions are balanced. Your spirit becomes free to be more present in your conscious life. Becoming this being of enlightened living can come along slowly or happen in an instant when you are ready.

Today is a good day to prepare yourself to become more aware of your true self. Many ways can lead to this awakening state. How can you do this? Can you let yourself be guided to fruition? Becoming aware of this possibility is an excellent first step. May you take the steps you need.

- Namaste -

When You Forget

You are brave ones who live on Earth and inhabit earthly forms. Your spirit and soul have agreed to become physical and learn the lessons that come with this life. You are brave even when you are afraid or sad, or angry. You do not give yourselves enough credit.

It is helpful to sit with yourself and let the negative thoughts pass like clouds going by in the sky. You can notice and observe them but then let them go by. When you have forgotten your goodness, bravery, and worth, it is helpful to sit or walk in nature and center yourself again. Speak words of caring and hope to yourself. Name your blessings. Give thanks for everything you have, from the small things to the infinite.

Today is a good day to be your own best friend. Take time to be good to yourself in healthy ways. Give thanks and spread the kindness you nurture in yourself to others.

- Namaste -

All That Is Offered

Participation in life is crucial and comes from your ability to balance the relationship between the physical and non-physical. As you draw energy from the universe, you can do many things previously undreamed. Daily life is not just the monotony of going from home to work to home again. Rather is a daily adventure that is uniquely yours. As you begin each day, it is helpful to gather the energy you need to get going and to remember that you are more than just a body going about your business. You are a being here to grow and learn, to help and share with others.

Today is a good day to start giving thanks and recognizing all that's being offered to you. Even as you go about driving, working, and relating to others, you are growing and deepening your skills. Giving thanks helps you realize the goodness and abundance you have manifested.

- Namaste -

The Anchor of Thankfulness

Peace comes when you become more aware of your true nature and how you live your life. All along your path come challenges and resulting moments of insight. You are constantly flowing and growing, learning and becoming more than you were. In each instance, there comes change. Because your life is so constructed, it is beneficial to accept that all you see, feel and think at this moment will change. The fear of this, the trying to keep things forever the same, leads to a lack of peace for yourself. This fear of change or loss of the familiar replaces calmness and kindness with negativity.

One way to help yourself is to seek out those things to be grateful for whenever possible. This anchors you to endless moments in your life. Then you are not so worried about the past and future.

Today is a good day to practice the skill of being grateful. As often as you can, bring it to mind. As you look at yourself, give thanks. If you become fearful, sit and focus on what good there is for you. Challenges tend to shrink in the light of thankfulness and gratitude.

- Namaste -

A Positive Force of Life

As a tolling bell sends out ripples of sound, you also send out energy beyond yourself into the void of the universe. Your thoughts, emotions, and words are forms of energy that you send out. Therefore, you must learn and practice the skills of self-regulation to be a buoyant transmitter of loving kindness to yourself and others through your thoughts, words, and actions.

You may wonder if you are that important, but you are more important than you realize. All of you are connected, and it is through your connections to all that you can be a force of positive energy. This is especially true in these times when many are afraid. You can be a support for calm and beneficial action.

Today is a good day to find your ways of relaxing and finding your calm state. This helps you to have the realization of your worth, which is excellent. As you seek this clear awareness, you will find it more often. Then you will influence others to do the same.

- Namaste -

Noticing

The many tiny plants and creatures that exist in the outside world around you are barely noticeable, yet they are plentiful and live in worlds that many do not even notice. Not noticing doesn't mean that. Your life is meant to be significant, but many don't realize how important their time is to them or others. Undervaluing or underestimating your worth and importance is a standard error. It would be beneficial if all children were taught their worth in their early days so that they know the actual value of their time.

It is good to sit with yourself and go within to explore yourself and your relationship to the universe. So much exists, not just in the physical realm but also in other domains. When you ask for support, you will receive it. Reminding yourself of the support available to you is essential. Then be humble enough to give thanks constantly as you become more aware of the goodness in your life. As you express this gratitude, you change your thoughts and emotions to a higher level of being, and your life will have more opportunities and insights.

Today is a good day to sit and reflect on your breath as you breathe in and out. As you become more relaxed, you are more open to examining your life. As you go about your day, you become better equipped to be kind to yourself and others. It is of benefit to expand your knowledge and your noticing of these small worlds within your world. Taking walks or just sitting in nature can assist you in noticing and perhaps appreciating more of the big picture of creation that surrounds you. Seeing the tiny creatures, plants, or even stones and rocks, helps develop an understanding of the world that is to your benefit and the benefit of others. This noticing also leads to better development of compassion. As you expand your awareness, you increase your ability to be kind, respectful, and tolerant of the differences you encounter.

Today is a good day to begin to train yourself to notice more of the world around you. Notice the different parts of the universe of creation that surround you. Notice and express gratitude for all you see.

- Namaste -

Examine Life

Your life is meant to be significant, but many don't realize how important their time is to them or others. Undervaluing or underestimating your worth and importance is a standard error. It would be beneficial if all children were taught their worth in their early days so that they know the actual value of their time. It is good to sit with yourself and go within to explore yourself and your relationship to the universe.

So much exists, not just in the physical realm but also in other domains. When you ask for support, you will receive it. Reminding yourself of the support available to you is essential. Then be humble enough to give thanks constantly as you become more aware of the goodness in your life. As you express this gratitude, you change your thoughts and emotions to a higher level of being, and your life will have more opportunities and insights.

Today is a good day to sit and reflect on your breath as you breathe in and out. As you become more relaxed, you are more open to examining your life. As you go about your day, you become better equipped to be kind to yourself and others.

- Namaste -

Chances to Grow

Repeating mistakes is a proven way to increase skills. Over time there tends to be a learning of skills to view your errors and mistakes differently. Instead of having a negative attitude towards them, you can cultivate more of a sense of curiosity about them. When you lessen the sting of making a mistake, you can change the patterns of thought and emotion that lead to them. In a sense, there are no mistakes, but perhaps different or more skillful choices can lead to more pleasing or healthier results.

Today is a good day to observe your choices as much as you can. This may come after the choice, during, or before. Be kind in how you treat yourself. View your choices not as right or wrong but as chances to grow.

- Namaste -

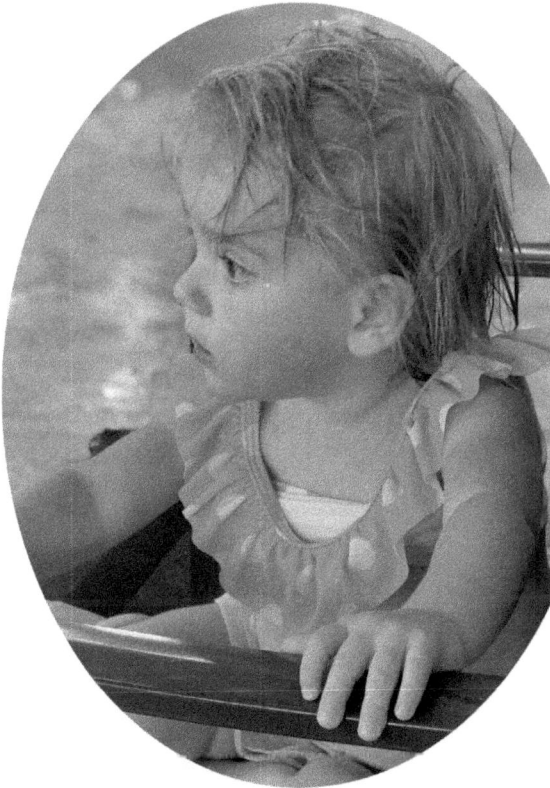

Sustenance

When you seek to sit in silence, you do a great service for yourself and those around you. When you sit and open yourself to receiving energy and inspiration, you become a light source for all around you. Your part here is to be a light source of healing, kindness, support, and comfort. You can only do this when you balance yourself and are open to the Source's love and support. The energy of the universe sustains you, and you can use it to help create a better place for yourself and others.

Today is a good day to refresh yourself in ways that work for you. As you care for yourself, you can be of caring to others. An empty well cannot quench anyone's thirst. Fill yourself with energy. Know that you help others when you help yourself. You are all connected. Spread loving energy whenever you can.

- Namaste -

Drawn to It

Water makes up so much of you that you cannot help but be drawn to it, attracted to it for your survival and beauty. It is beneficial to sit by the water, be it a lake, a river, a stream, or a pool. The ocean is also a powerful spot for you to find your connection.

Water is a blessing whether it falls as rain or you drink it to quench your thirst. Water is a physical necessity and promotes your vision of life. When you sit beside water, listen to its melody of sound. Is it a running through the rocks sound? Is it a waterfall sound? Is it waves, large or small? Is it the splashing of bodies enjoying its refreshingness? Is it the tears of emotion that cleanse you?

Today is a good day to observe all the water you see, hear, taste, and feel. Give thanks for its showers of blessings in your life. Give thanks, as it sustains you in many ways.

- Namaste -

Emotional Maps

Your emotions are meant to help you along your way. They are little signs that point you in the right direction to go. Your ability to progress is often supported by paying attention to these signs that line your path, your road. Some are small. Some come in larger versions, but they all have information that can aid you in finding your way.

Sometimes, it may seem improper to have these emotions, so you might add shame to them. "I should not feel this. I am not okay if I do. Others will judge me." And so you judge yourself.

It is helpful to develop the skill to observe your emotional messages rather than judge them. You might even say, "Oh, I am judging this emotion." When you can feel and observe it, you have a complete message that can help you follow the map of yourself

Today is a good day to feel, recognize and bless all of your feelings. What message do they have for you? How can they be of benefit? Know that this skill of recognition, observation, and acceptance takes practice. Love yourself for being willing to learn and grow.

Namaste

It's Just the Weather

Your personal weather is like a system that is contained around and within you. This system keeps changing all of the time. In it is contained your individualized microcosm of energy. Much like the weather outside your window, there's constantly dynamic movement of energy. Sometimes you feel sunny and happy. Your energy, thoughts, emotions, and actions are accessible. Things seem clear and perhaps warm and comfortable.

Then sometimes, you may experience a gathering of clouds and feel your energy like the gathering before a storm. You may feel your thoughts and emotions become more turbulent. There may even be stormy conditions with energy bolts and thundering emotions and actions. Then may come the cleansing tears that fall like raindrops, releasing you from the drought of sadness, sorrow, or regret. And then that stormy system moves on to leave things refreshed. Wherever you find yourself, be it sunny days or stormy weather, know that you grow and learn from your experience. It is just the weather.

Today is a good day to observe your personal weather system. Notice its changes, and be aware of how you are perhaps being nurtured or impacted. Notice any patterns contained in it. Express gratitude for being alive.

- Namaste -

Like A Flower

All of you are growing each day. Even if you are unaware, you are expanding and becoming more of a channel of love and light.

As you become more filled with this Source of energy and your awareness grows, you can better give to and accept the love of all.

Much benefits from your opening, like the beautiful flowers on Earth. Like the flowers, you grow from a tiny seed, bursting forth from the Earth, growing into the young you and reaching towards your maturity. Then, you blossom with beauty and purpose when the time is right. You give to the world the purpose of your being. The fragrance, the color, and the pollen of your work spread to others, and you are a joy. When you are in later life, your buds lose their vibrancy, slowly falling and dying back, but like all perennials, your next season is hidden in the garden to germinate, grow and flower again.

Today is a good day to notice about you all the color and vibrancy. You are a part of this beautiful landscape. Cultivate your gratefulness for all the beauty that comes to you.

- Namaste -

Walking Together

Make way for the parade of good and loving beings that want to walk with you. Many other souls seek to be with you in this time period. They desire to walk as though in a parade, holding your hand in friendship and showing others the goodness that comes from forming connections.

Just as in a parade, the more diverse it is, the more successful it is. Seeing all the new and creative ways of expression is thrilling. The open mind and heart clap with delight when seeing and feeling the significant number of souls holding hands to walk together. Young and old benefit from this coming together to celebrate life.

Today is a good day to look at yourself and notice this parade of experiences and opportunities that comes to you. Welcome them and be grateful whether they are familiar or something different. The world is a great parade of learning and growth.

- Namaste -

About the Author

Dianne Larsen is a retired social worker living in a small Iowa town with her husband, Mike. Her vision quest for spiritual truth and understanding led her to explore Paganism, Christianity, Buddhism, and the physical disciplines of Yoga, Tai Chi, and Qigong. Early on, she visited Findhorn Village in Scotland, the spiritual community renowned as a magical place for quiet contemplation, meditation, singing, and learning. For a time, she studied with Native American medicine man, Sun Bear, at Vision Mountain outside Spokane, Washington.